uide

Oban, Mull
and Kintyre

W A L K S

*Compiled by
Brian Conduit,
John Brooks and Hugh Taylor*

JARROLD
publishing

Acknowledgements
My thanks for the invaluable advice and useful leaflets
obtained from the various tourist information centres
throughout the area, and in particular to Ian Everard of Forest
Enterprise for assisting me with the route for the Beinn Bheula
walk and for contributing the article on the Argyll Forest Park.

Text:	Brian Conduit, John Brooks, Hugh Taylor
Photography:	Brian Conduit, John Brooks, Hugh Taylor
Editorial:	Ark Creative, Norwich
Design:	Ark Creative, Norwich

Series Consultant: Brian Conduit

© Jarrold Publishing, an imprint of Pitkin Publishing Ltd

Jarrold Publishing

ISBN 978-0-7117-0992-8

While every care has been taken to ensure the accuracy of the
route directions, the publishers cannot accept responsibility for
errors or omissions, or for changes in details given. The
countryside is not static: hedges and fences can be removed,
field boundaries can alter, footpaths can be rerouted and
changes in ownership can result in the closure or diversion of
some concessionary paths. Also, paths that are easy and
pleasant for walking in fine conditions may become slippery,
muddy and difficult in wet weather, while stepping stones
across rivers and streams may become impassable.
    If you find an inaccuracy in either the text or maps, please
write to or e-mail Jarrold Publishing at the addresses below.

First published 1998
Reprinted 2004, 2006.

Printed in Belgium. 4/07

Pitkin Publishing Ltd
Healey House, Dene Road, Andover, Hampshire SP10 2AA
email: info@totalwalking.co.uk
www. totalwalking.co.uk

Front cover: Colourful Tobermory
Previous page: Oban, the 'Gateway to the Isles'

Contents

The Law and Tradition as they affect Walking in Scotland; Scotland's Hills and Mountains: a Concordat on Access; Safety on the Hills; Glossary of Gaelic names; Useful Organisations; Ordnance Survey Maps

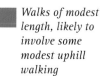

Short, easy walks

Walks of modest length, likely to involve some modest uphill walking

More challenging walks which may be longer and/or over more rugged terrain, often with some stiff climbs

Keymap 1

SCALE 1:384 615 or 1 INCH to about 6 MILES *1CM to 3.8KM*

0 2 4 6 8 10 KILOMETRES 15

0 2 4 MILES 8 10

KEYMAP HEIGHTS SHOWN IN FEET

Keymap 2

Walk	Page	Start	Nat. Grid Reference	Distance	Time	Highest Point
Ardcastle Wood	52	Ardcastle Wood	NR 940920	5 miles (8km)	3 hrs	259ft (79m)
Ardmore and Glengorm	61	Ardmore car park	NM 485557	8 miles (12.9km)	4 hrs	525ft (160m)
Beinn Bheula	79	Glenbranter	NS 109975	9½ miles (15.3km)	6 hrs	2556ft (779m)
Beinn Lora	42	Benderloch	NM 905381	4 miles (6.4km)	2 hrs	1010ft (308m)
The Ben Cruachan Horseshoe	82	Cruachan power station	NN 076269	8 miles (12.9km)	8 hrs	3694ft (1126m)
Ben More	87	On shores of Loch na Keal	NM 494359	6 miles (9.7km)	5 hrs	3171ft (966m)
Bowmore and Loch Indaal	67	Bowmore	NR 310599	8½ miles (13.7km)	4 hrs	98ft (30m)
Campbeltown Loch	30	Campbeltown	NR 721204	4½ miles (7.2km)	2 hrs	623ft (190m)
Carradale	64	Port na Storm car park	NR 811383	7½ miles (12.1km)	4 hrs	756ft (230m)
Clachan of Glendaruel and Kilmodan Stones	26	Glendaruel Caravan Park	NS 000869	4¾ miles (7.6km)	2½ hrs	129ft (39m)
Connel and the Black Lochs	44	Connel	NM 915340	5½ miles (8.9km)	3 hrs	213ft (65m)
Crinan Canal and Knapdale Forest	74	Crinan	NR 788941	9 miles (14.5km)	4 hrs	705ft (214m)
Dalmally and Monument Hill	20	Dalmally	NN 159271	4 miles (6.4km)	2 hrs	525ft (160m)
Dùn na Cuaiche, Inveraray	40	Inveraray Castle	NN 096093	2½ miles (4km)	2 hrs	755ft (230m)
Garmony Point and the Fishnish Peninsula	50	Garmony car park	NM 661423	7 miles (11.3km)	3 hrs	131ft (40m)
Inverinan Glen	18	Inverinan Glen car park	NM 997175	3 miles (4.8km)	1½ hrs	410ft (125m)
Isle of Iona	70	Iona, by ferry terminal	NM 286240	8½ miles (13.7km)	4½ hrs	333ft (101m)
Isle of Kerrera	47	Kerrera Jetty	NM 830286	6 miles (9.7km)	3½ hrs	328ft (100m)
Isle of Lismore	35	Achnacroish	NM 852409	4½ miles (7.2km)	2½ hrs	164ft (50m)
Isle of Ulva	58	Ulva, Boathouse Visitor Centre	NM 443397	7½ miles (12.1km)	4 hrs	328ft (100m)
Kames to Millhouse on the Cowal Way	16	Kames	NR 979700	3½ miles (5.6km)	2 hrs	263ft (80m)
Loch Avich	38	Dalavich, on north-west shore of Loch Awe	NM 970139	5 miles (8km)	2½ hrs	492ft (150m)
Oban and Pulpit Hill	24	Oban	NM 834282	4 miles (6.4km)	2 hrs	230ft (70m)
Port Askaig and Ballygrant	55	Port Askaig	NR 431692	7½ miles (12.1km)	3½ hrs	240ft (73m)
Portavadie and Low Stillaig	14	Portavadie	NR 932691	3¼ miles (5.2km)	2 hrs	221ft (67m)
Salen	32	Salen	NM 572431	4 miles (6.4km)	2 hrs	427ft (130m)
Tobermory and Aros Park	28	Ledaig car park	NM 504551	4½ miles (7.2km)	2½ hrs	213ft (65m)
The Wishing Tree and Kilchoan Bay	22	By entrance to Ardmaddy Castle	NM 791169	4½ miles (7.2km)	2 hrs	558ft (170m)

Comments

There is a choice of waymarked routes through the forest here, all of them giving splendid views over Loch Fyne. Keep your eyes peeled as you walk along the shore, as this is a favourite haunt of otters.

A mainly forest walk near the lonely north coast of Mull, with grand views across the water to the rugged Ardnamurchan peninsula.

There are forest tracks and much rough hill and moorland walking on this ascent of Beinn Bheula. The views, especially from the summit, are superb and extensive.

A short but quite steep climb through forest to the summit of Beinn Lora rewards you with a magnificent all-round view.

This route should only be attempted by fit, competent walkers as the total height climbed in the traverse exceeds 5000ft (1524m). Some agility is needed to negotiate exposed rock-slabs and gullies.

A steady and unremitting climb to the highest peak on Mull rewards you with magnificent panoramic views over mountains, islands and sea lochs.

This is a generally flat and easy walk. The first part, near the shores of Loch Indaal, has fine views across the loch; later come imposing views of the Paps of Jura on the horizon.

From the forested slopes of Beinn Ghuilean above Campbeltown Loch, the views over Kintyre are outstanding.

On this combination of coastal, woodland and moorland walking, there are fine views over Kintyre and across Kilbrannan Sound to the isle of Arran.

This is a walk along an ancient byway through some of the finest rural scenery in Argyll. An old church, a collection of carved stones and a superb bowl of soup at the end all serve to enhance the magic.

The route passes by the Black Lochs of Kilvaree, a trio of lonely and mysterious-looking lochs to the south of Loch Etive.

Flat walking at the start and finish beside the lovely Crinan Canal contrasts with a hillier middle stretch through forest.

An easy walk along a track leads to a monument and a magnificent viewpoint near the head of Loch Awe.

The short climb up to this knoll gives grand views over Loch Fyne. However in bygone days it was the view into the mouths of the three nearby glens that made it important to the Campbell lookouts.

There are fine views across the Sound of Mull to the cliffs and hills of Morvern on this easy walk across marshland and through forest.

This fairly easy and highly enjoyable route features attractive woodland walking around the gorge of the River Inan, plus fine views over Loch Awe.

There is immense historical interest and a wealth of ancient monuments, as well as grand views and superb beaches, on this atmospheric walk on the holy isle of Iona.

Kerrera has a special romantic atmosphere and this makes the effort of getting there worthwhile. Its scenery is wild and beautiful, with the ruined Gylen Castle adding to the romance.

From this long and flat island in the middle of Loch Linnhe there are fine views in all directions. The route passes the former cathedral of the bishops of Argyll.

A fascinating walk, with some impressive coastal views, on a remote and thinly populated island that has no roads or cars.

This walk follows the line of a long distance footpath and a right of way once used to ferry high explosives at a time when this sleepy backwater was a major centre of industry.

The switchback nature of this forest walk is not apparent from the map, and may surprise the unwary. However the energy expended proves worthwhile when you reach the lonely shore of Loch Avich.

A low level outward route is followed by a higher level return, with magnificent views across Oban Bay from Pulpit Hill.

After a short coastal stretch above the Sound of Islay, followed by some road walking, the remainder of the route is through lovely lochside woodlands.

Two abandoned settlements and awesome sea views are the highlights of this walk. One of the villages was a typical 18th century settlement where subsistence agriculture was the mainstay.

This walk near the east coast of Mull includes woodland and rough moorland and gives some fine views over the Sound of Mull and Loch na Keal.

There are grand views across Tobermory Bay and an interesting circuit of Aros Park, with its fine woodland, display of rhododendrons, waterfalls and lochan.

There are grand coastal views, especially over Kilchoan Bay and Seil Sound, and the route passes by an unusual tree.

Introduction to Oban, Mull and Kintyre

A few miles to the north of Lochgilphead, overlooking the flat and marshy Mòine Mhór, the Great Moss, is the rock of Dunadd, site of a prehistoric fort. This rock can claim not only to be the first capital of Scotland but also the birthplace of Scotland, for it was here that the Scots established their headquarters after landing from Ireland on the nearby west coast around AD500. Dunadd became the capital of their kingdom of Dalriada and it was the later union of Scots and native Picts under Kenneth McAlpin that created the first Scottish kingdom.

Dunadd stands at the heart of the ancient kingdom – and the present administrative division – of Argyll, which roughly corresponds to the area covered by this walking guide. To the north is Oban and the high rugged hills, narrow glens and long sinewy lochs of the Western Highlands. To the south the narrow finger of the Kintyre Peninsula stretches down to Campbeltown and the Mull of Kintyre, the latter within sight of the Antrim coast of Northern Ireland and on roughly the same latitude as Alnwick in Northumberland. To the east across the long inlet of Loch Fyne are the hills and forests of the Cowal Peninsula, bounded by Loch Long and the Firth of Clyde. To the west is the coast, and beyond it the islands of the Inner Hebrides – Islay, Jura, Mull and countless smaller ones.

Most visitors approach this area from the south, either taking the road northwards from Glasgow via Loch Lomond, or getting one of the ferries across the Firth of Clyde from Gourock to Dunoon. The latter route is an excellent introduction to the region. As soon as the ferry leaves Gourock on industrial Clydeside, the view ahead is one of high wooded hills and long sea lochs, the start of the Highlands.

From Dunoon, chief town of Cowal, the main road leads northwards, through the Argyll Forest Park and along the shores of Loch Eck and Loch Fyne to Inveraray, overlooked by the castle of the dukes of Argyll. Continuing northwards, you come to the head of Loch Awe. Here you turn westwards, passing through the dramatic Pass of Brander and below mighty Ben Cruachan, to the shores of Loch Etive. A short drive along the coastline of the Lynn of Lorne brings you to Oban, principal town and major ferry port of the Western Highlands. Oban is an excellent walking centre, with a variety of coast, hill, woodland and lochside walks within very easy reach of the town. It is also the springboard for walks on some of the islands.

From Oban's bustling harbour, the ubiquitous Caledonian MacBrayne ferries sail to many of the islands of the Inner Hebrides. The most regular crossings are to Mull, about 40 minutes away, whose mountain profile, dominated inevitably by Ben More, becomes increasingly more impressive as the ferry passes Duart Castle, ancestral home of the MacLean Clan, and approaches the terminal at Craignure.

Lismore church, the choir of the 13th-century cathedral

Mull is one of the largest and most mountainous islands in the Hebrides, and possesses in Ben More the only Munro (peak of 3000ft (914m) or more) in the island group outside Skye. It also has a long, majestic and varied coastline, and Loch na Keal, overlooked by Ben More, almost cuts the island in two. The capital and only town is Tobermory, located in the north-east corner, its brightly painted buildings attractively grouped around one of the most sheltered harbours in the area.

Some of the smaller and flatter islands that lie off Mull or Oban should not be ignored. The sparsely populated isles of Kerrera and Ulva are both worth exploring and on no account should you omit to visit Lismore and Iona, both highly attractive and ancient religious centres with churches that were formerly cathedrals. The unique religious significance of Iona – and its unrivalled collection of ecclesiastical monuments – attract visitors from all over the world, and it is no more than a ten-minute ferry crossing from Fionnphort at the south-western tip of the Ross of Mull.

Inveraray lies at an important junction of roads. As well as the road that heads northwards to Oban, another one leads south-westwards, following the shore of Loch Fyne to Lochgilphead. Near here the beautiful, nine-mile (14.5km) long Crinan Canal cuts across the narrow neck of Knapdale to Crinan on the west coast. This was Scotland's equivalent of the Panama Canal, built in the late 18th century to avoid the long and often stormy journey around the Mull of Kintyre.

The road then turns south to the delightful fishing port of Tarbert, located at the even narrower neck of the Kintyre Peninsula, and continues down the west coast of Kintyre before turning eastwards to Campbeltown. Situated at the head of a sheltered loch, this is the largest town for miles around. A little further south is the Mull of Kintyre, the tip of the peninsula. Because of its relative inaccessibility, Kintyre is not as well known as it deserves and remains delightfully unspoilt with heather-clad hills, lush glens, a fine coastline and imposing views across Kilbrannan Sound to the mountains of Arran.

From Kennacraig on the outstandingly beautiful West Loch Tarbert, ferries cross to Islay and the adjacent isle of Jura. Both are among the larger Hebridean islands, but here the similarity ends. Whereas Islay is mainly flat, has several small towns and villages and a flourishing whisky industry, Jura is a rugged, mountainous and virtually uninhabited wilderness, its skyline dominated by the distinctive rounded peaks of the three Paps, a major landmark over much of the Inner Hebrides and west coast of Scotland.

Loch na Keal

Whether on the mainland of Argyll around Oban, farther south on the Cowal and Kintyre peninsulas, or on Mull and some of the other islands, this region offers some of the finest walking to be found anywhere in Britain, with a series of majestic and varied landscapes. Water is almost always an element as the walks are never far from an inland loch, sea loch or the coast. Hills are inevitably an ever-present feature, either near at hand or on the distant horizon, and there are many forests throughout the area where you can walk some of the Forestry Commission's well-waymarked trails.

Sensible precautions will enable you to enjoy the walks in safety. Keep a careful eye on the weather, especially if going out on to the hills, and be prepared to modify your walk if there is a deterioration. Always take adequate clothing and appropriate footwear. Choose walks where both the terrain and length are suitable for you. Most of the walks in this guide should be well within the capabilities of the average walker, except perhaps for walks 26-28 which involve some fairly strenuous climbing across rough country. *Take particular care in winter and on no account try to tackle these last three walks unless you are experienced in hill walking in bad conditions and able to navigate by using a compass.*

From August onwards when grouse-shooting and deer-stalking take place on the hills and moors, some of the walks may be restricted or closed at times. During this period it is best to check with the local tourist information centre or estate office.

One last piece of advice. If intending to go walking on some of the islands – one of the delights of the region and thoroughly recommended – you will immediately become aware of the importance of the ferries – the lifeblood of the islands and their chief link with the mainland. As the frequency of ferry services varies enormously from one island to another, it is essential to acquire and carefully study the current Caledonian MacBrayne timetable before planning your trip.

Argyll Forest Park

Created in 1935, the Argyll Forest Park was the first Forest Park to be established in Britain. The park includes much of the Arrochar Alps and the high ground and loch-sides of the eastern side of the Cowal Peninsula.

Although the Forestry Commission's primary purpose was to grow timber, it also provided recreation. Being only 40 miles (64km) from Glasgow, half of Scotland's population live within 65 miles (105km) of the Forest Park, making it highly accessible to many people.

Walking in the Forest Park, the variety of terrain provides routes of all types, from easy coastal walks to challenging hill walking. Walkers in the Park may well get a rare glimpse of the golden eagle (the Forest Park emblem), as well as the chance to see red and roe deer in the forest or on the open hill. Amongst the broadleaved woodlands at Glenbranter and Loch Eckside, the rich habitat provides homes for redstarts, wood warblers and many small birds attracted by the insects in the bluebell woods.

Many conifer areas, particularly around Puck's Glen forest walk, contain other woodland wildlife that requires a quick eye to spot, such as red squirrels and occasionally foxes.

With a wide range of hills and glens, the walking can be varied and interesting. With many small tops being rarely visited, do not always expect to meet fellow walkers on the hills. The white post system is designed to help indicate access to the hills, but once beyond the forest fence, the map and compass need to be used. White posts appear at all hill accesses either on the forest roads or the point where they cross the forest fence, enabling the walker to find easy access to the open hill.

Contributed by Ian Everard

Environment Forester,
Forest Enterprise, Cowal
Forest District

Glenbranter from Beinn Bheula

Introduction

Portavadie and Low Stillaig

Start	Portavadie
Distance	3¼ miles (5.2km)
Approximate time	2 hours
Parking	At start
Refreshments	Hotels and tearooms in Kames and Tighnabruich
Ordnance Survey maps	Landranger 62 (North Kintyre & Tarbert), Explorer 362 (Cowal West & Isle of Bute)

As well as superb views across Loch Fyne to the Kintyre Peninsula and the Island of Arran this short walk passes several millennia of Scottish History. From the multi-million pound white elephant at Pollphail village past Bronze Age standing stones and a farm settlement of the 18th century the attempts of humans to settle in this remote corner may be visible but have made little impact.

Park on the roadside just past the turning to the ferry and before the sign declaring 'End of Public Road'. From here you can head along a narrow road following the Scottish Rights of Way Society sign for Portavadie and Low Stillaig Walk. Pass by a waymarker to the right of a decrepit gate, ignoring the 'danger keep out sign', and continue along a concrete road passing the moldering settlement on your right.

This is Pollphail built by the

Government to house construction workers in the mid-1970s. Over £11 million of taxpayers' money was poured into the construction of this and a nearby dry dock. The intention was to create employment by building oil platforms for the North Sea but unsurprisingly it won no orders. Civil servants seemed to have overlooked the fact that it was on the wrong side of the country, served by inadequate roads and an almost total lack of local labour.

When the road bends keep straight ahead following waymarker arrows to climb some wooden steps on the left. Then turn left and follow the path to another set of steps before heading uphill through woodland to reach open hillside by another marker **A**. Pause here to admire the views back across the ruins. Then veer right and continue following a faint path uphill. In late spring and summer look out for the Heath Spotted Orchids which grow here.

At the top of the hill turn right at a waymarker and go downhill on a clearly

Abandoned settlement, Low Stillaig

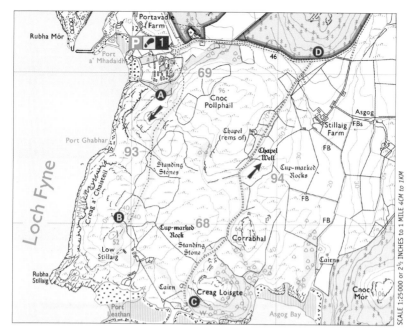

visible path that you will see stretching into the distance. This section is very boggy particularly after prolonged periods of rain. The worst parts are crossed by duckboards. Look out for bog cotton growing through the heather.

Go through a gap in an earthen enclosure by another marker and turn right. At the next marker, stop to enjoy the views across Loch Fyne. Below you are the rings of one of many fish farms operating in the Loch and beyond that the Kintyre Peninsula and the village of Tarbert which can be reached by ferry from Portavadie. Continuing on the walk you should see the island of Arran and Goat Fell – its highest mountain.

Continue following the path as it curves towards the loch to pass two standing stones. Soon the path widens to a track. When this forks **B** keep right to reach the ruins of Low Stillaig. This abandoned township is typical of the settlements that existed throughout Cowal in the 18th century. They would have supported several families who would live almost entirely on the potatoes, oats and barley grown on the settlement.

Turn left from the ruins and head east to pick up a waymarker. Pass this to reach a track then cross a bridge over the burn and turn right onto a track which will eventually become a grassy path. Keep on this to reach a marker **C** near a Boys' Brigade Outdoor Centre. Turn left onto a well surfaced track.

Follow this to another standing stone which may have been used in conjunction with the two passed earlier as an early form of calendar to determine the best crop planting times.

In a little over ½ mile (800m) along this road if you poke about in the heather to the left of the road you might come across the turf foundations of an ancient chapel. They are within a turf walled enclosure. This is early Christian and was perhaps occupied by an early follower of St. Columba.

From here follow the track to the main road **D**, turn left at the drive for the award-winning Glendaruel Caravan Park **D**, then follow it to the start of the walk. ●

Kames to Millhouse on the Cowal Way

Start	Kames
Distance	3½ miles (5.6km)
Approximate time	2 hours
Parking	Car park near tank landing jetty
Refreshments	Cranachan Tearoom Tighnabruich
Ordnance Survey maps	Landranger 62 (North Kintyre & Tarbert), Explorer 362 (Cowal West & Isle of Bute)

Another short and easy walk with splendid views over the Kyles of Bute, one of the most beautiful spots in Scotland. The first half of the walk traces a route that was used daily to transport cartloads of gunpowder from the mills in Kames to the central magazine for storage.

Start from the tank landing car park and follow the sign for the public footpath to 'Millhouse via the golf course'.

Follow the distinctive red waymarkers of the Cowal way onto a footpath leading uphill through woodland. This can be very boggy in wet weather and suitable footwear is a must.

This is part of the old right of way used to transport gunpowder from Kames to the storage magazine and back again for shipping. It was known locally as the Green Road because a top layer of turf was put on the surface to avoid sparks being caused by the horses' shoes hitting the stones. At the peak of production some 70 cart loads of gunpowder were being hauled along this road every day with coal, charcoal, sulphur and saltpetre forming the return load.

When the path ends at a T-junction. Ⓐ turn right onto a track. When the track forks Ⓑ keep left onto an overgrown track. When this comes to an end carefully cross the golf course. The way ahead is blocked by gorse so turn right and follow the edge of the gorse to reach the end. Then turn left, go through a gate in the fence and turn left again heading uphill through a boggy section to regain the track. Turn right and continue along it, following the line of the fence all the way to the road. This is an exceedingly boggy section. To your right are the remains of the former gunpowder magazine.

This remote corner of Argyll was chosen to become Scotland's largest gunpowder manufacturing facility because it was far removed from the main centre of population. Work started in 1839 and between then and 1921 in excess of 400 people earned their living in the factories producing up to 4000 tons of explosives each year.

Cross a stile by a lodge and the Dolphin Bell Ⓒ then turn right onto the road. The former timekeeping bell from

On the Cowal Way to Millhouse

the factory in Millhouse was renovated and erected here in 2000 and now forms part of a memorial to the 16 workers who lost their lives making the black powder. One, John McGilp, died in 1922 during the dismantling of the works. Four other names appear on the memorial. They were part of the crew of the appropriately named works steamer *Guy Fawkes* who drowned when it sank in 1864.

Follow this road back to Kames and when it turns sharp left keep ahead, following it round to the right then turn left and head downhill, passing the Kames Hotel, to reach the shore. Turn left and follow the shore road back to the car park. Walking along this final stretch it's difficult to imagine that this was once a thriving industrial centre. Few signs remain. After the gunpowder factories, Kames reverted to a sleepy seaside village. ●

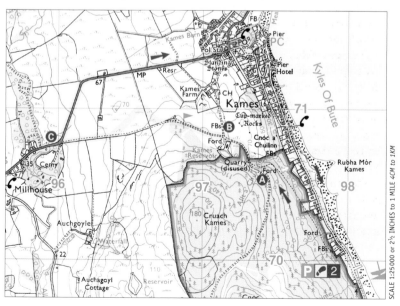

Inverinan Glen

Start	Inverinan, Forestry Commission's Inverinan Glen car park
Distance	3 miles (4.8km)
Approximate time	1½ hours
Parking	Inverinan Glen
Refreshments	None
Ordnance Survey maps	Landranger 55 (Lochgilphead & Loch Awe), Explorer 360 (Loch Awe & Inveraray)

This short, pleasant and easy walk takes you through the attractive mixed woodlands surrounding the gorge of the River Inan (Abhainn Fionain) and some of its tributary burns. At one stage you pass a waterfall and there are some very good views over Loch Awe.

🖉 Turn right out of the car park along the road, and at a Forestry Commission footpath sign to Inverinan Glen turn left on to a gently ascending path. For the whole of this route you follow red footprint waymarks.

On the edge of the trees, bear left and climb steadily to enter the forest, a mixture of broadleaved trees and conifers. Look out for where a yellow arrow directs you to turn left Ⓐ and

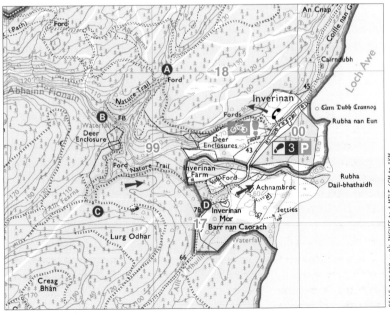

Inverinan Glen

head down to ford a tributary burn, Allt a' Chreagain.

Continue uphill, emerging into a more open area of felled woodland, and at a fork take the left-hand path that runs along the right edge of the trees.

The path bends right, then descends gently, then after a left turn it continues more steeply downhill.

Turn sharp right to cross a footbridge over the River Inan by a waterfall **B**, a lovely spot. On the other side of the bridge, the path curves left and winds through an area of most attractive woodland to reach a broad track. Turn left here – the remainder of the walk follows a cycle route.

Take the first turning on the left **C**, follow a path gently downhill to emerge from the trees and continue along a track which keeps along the left edge of the forest. From here there are fine views ahead over Loch Awe.

The track curves right to a road **D**. Turn left, descend to cross a bridge over the river and follow the road back to the starting point of the walk at the Inverninan Glen car park.

Dalmally and Monument Hill

Start	Dalmally
Distance	4 miles (6.4km) Shorter version 2½ miles (4km)
Approximate time	2 hours (1½ hours for shorter walk)
Parking	Dalmally, station car park
Refreshments	Hotels at Dalmally
Ordnance Survey maps	Landranger 50 (Glen Orchy & Loch Etive), Explorers 360 (Loch Awe & Inveraray) and 377 (Loch Etive & Glen Orchy)

An easy and steady climb along a tarmac track through forest, from the village of Dalmally to a hilltop monument, rewards you with majestic and extensive views over the Strath of Orchy, Ben Cruachan, Loch Awe and the surrounding mountains and forests. The full walk takes you down through the village to Dalmally church, which occupies a fine position above the River Orchy.

Loch Awe from Monument Hill

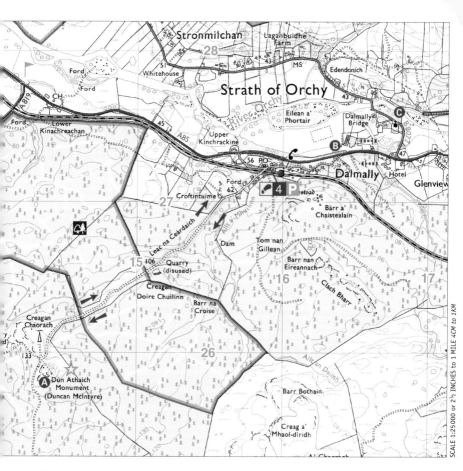

Dalmally has a superb location in the Strath of Orchy near the head of Loch Awe.

 From the station car park turn left uphill and bear left along a country lane signposted 'Monument Hill and Duncan Ban's Monument'.

Cross a railway bridge and follow the lane, once part of an old routeway between Dalmally and Inveraray, steadily uphill for 1½ miles (2.4km).

This attractive track, tree-lined at times, gives fine views over the mountains to the right, later passes between conifers and ends just below the monument. Turn left, head up the footpath to reach it **A** and take in the magnificent all-round views over lochs, mountains and forests. The views to the west are particularly impressive, looking along the length of the islet-studded Loch Awe, with Kilchurn Castle visible near the head of the loch and Ben Cruachan towering above its northern shores. The monument is to Duncan Ban MacIntyre, one of Scotland's finest Gaelic poets, who was born nearby in 1724 and died in Edinburgh in 1812.

For the shorter walk, retrace your steps downhill to the start.

For the full walk, carry on downhill through the village to the main road **B**, turn right and take the first turning on the left to the attractive, octagonal, early 19th-century church above the River Orchy **C**. Beyond the church is an elegant 18th-century bridge over the river. Retrace your steps uphill back to the station car park. ●

The Wishing Tree and Kilchoan Bay

Start	By entrance to Ardmaddy Castle grounds at end of minor road that leads south from the B844, 2½ miles (4km) south-west of Kilninver
Distance	4½ miles (7.2km)
Approximate time	2 hours
Parking	Beside track just beyond entrance to Ardmaddy Castle
Refreshments	None
Ordnance Survey maps	Landranger 55 (Lochgilphead & Loch Awe), Explorer 359 (Oban, Kerrera & Loch Melfort)

This 'there and back' walk follows a clear, easy and undulating track, once part of an old routeway between Oban and Loch Melfort, from the entrance to Ardmaddy Castle to a fine viewpoint above Kilchoan Bay. En route you pass the unusual Wishing Tree. There are some outstanding views across Seil Sound to the islands of Seil and Luing.

The walk begins by the entrance to the grounds of Ardmaddy Castle, which are sometimes open to the public. The castle is based around a late medieval tower-house, but was rebuilt in the 18th century and considerably enlarged in the 19th century.

Go through a gate and walk along a track, initially by conifers on the right, heading gently uphill. Descend to a gate, go through the gate and cross a bridge over a burn, Eas nan Ceardach. The remainder of the walk is across attractive open country.

Keep along the winding and undulating track, going through two metal gates and enjoying the fine views to the right across Seil Sound to the island of Seil.

After the second gate, the track bears left and climbs to the top of a pass, passing the remains of a solitary hawthorn that is known as the Wishing Tree Ⓐ. The

The Wishing Tree

trunk and branches of the tree are covered with coins, inserted by people who thought that it would make their dreams come true. The practice continues to this day but it has not done much for the tree which now lies dead within a wire enclosure.

From the top of the pass keep ahead, go through another metal gate and then continue across pleasant heathery moorland to the point at which the track starts to descend to the shores of Kilchoan Bay **B**. From this vantage point there is a glorious view ahead across the bay and Loch Melfort to the Craignish Peninsula and the small islands of Luing and Shuna.

From here retrace your steps to the start or, if you wish to extend the walk, you can continue down to the loch and return from there. ●

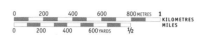

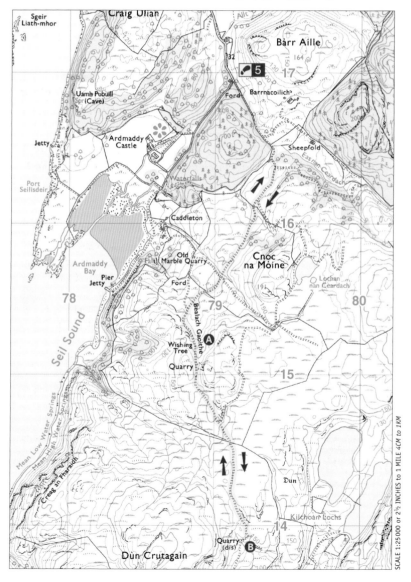

Oban and Pulpit Hill

Start	Oban
Distance	4 miles (6.4km)
Approximate time	2 hours
Parking	Oban
Refreshments	Pubs and cafés at Oban
Ordnance Survey maps	Landranger 49 (Oban & East Mull), Explorers 359 (Oban, Kerrera & Loch Melfort) and 376 (Oban & North Lorn)

The walk begins by heading southwards from Oban along the shores of the Sound of Kerrera as far as the ferry terminal for Kerrera. From there an easy climb leads on to the cliff above and you continue to Pulpit Hill, a superb viewpoint overlooking Oban Bay and harbour and the islands of Kerrera and Mull. A short descent then leads back to the start.

Oban, the 'Gateway to the Isles', splendidly situated on a large, crescent-shaped, sheltered bay, is the main town of the Western Highlands and a major tourist centre with a wide selection of shops, hotels, guest houses, pubs, and restaurants. Solid-looking Victorian buildings line the waterfront, and from its busy harbour, ferries can be taken to a large proportion of the Hebridean

Oban Bay and harbour

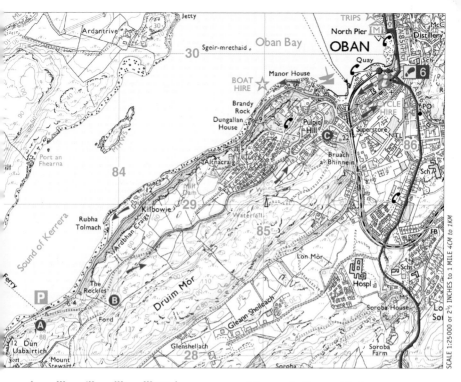

| 0 | 200 | 400 | 600 | 800 METRES | 1 |
| 0 | 200 | 400 | 600 YARDS | ½ | |

KILOMETRES
MILES

islands, large and small. Dominating the skyline is an imposing structure that looks like a replica of the Colosseum in Rome. This is McCaig's Tower, built between 1895 and 1900 to provide much-needed work for unemployed local stonemasons.

🖊 The walk starts in Argyll Square. Facing the harbour, turn left along Albany Street, cross a railway bridge and follow the road as it curves right, in the Gallanach direction. Keep along this quiet road for the next $1\frac{1}{2}$ miles (2.4km), alongside the Sound of Kerrera and below the steep wooded cliffs of Ardbhan Craigs.

At the Kerrera ferry terminal, turn sharp left **A** and head uphill along a grassy track to a metal gate. Go through, bear left across an area of rough grass – this part of the walk may be wet and muddy – to join a track **B** and continue along it. From now on,

conditions underfoot rapidly improve. The track eventually emerges on to a road on the edge of Oban. Turn right, at a T-junction turn left along a road signposted to Pulpit Hill, and where the main road bends left, keep ahead, still in the Pulpit Hill direction, to reach a car park and picnic area **C**.

A toposcope indicates all the places that can be seen from this magnificent vantage point 230ft (70m) above Oban harbour. They include Dunollie Castle on the opposite side of the bay, and the islands of Kerrera, Mull and Lismore.

In the far right-hand corner of the grassy area, go down steps and continue downhill along a tarmac path to a road. Turn left, take the downhill track ahead, which bisects two roads, to reach another road and keep ahead. Where the road bends right, turn left down a steeply descending tarmac path (Haggarts Brae) to a road at a bend. Turn half-right down to a junction, and keep ahead, crossing a railway bridge, to return to the start.

Clachan of Glendaruel and Kilmodan Carved Stones

Start	Glendaruel Caravan Park
Distance	4¾ miles (7.6km)
Approximate time	2½ hours
Parking	Glendaruel Caravan Park
Refreshments	Tearoom at Caravan Park and hotel at Clachan of Glendaruel
Ordnance Survey maps	Landranger 62 (North Kintyre & Tarbert), Explorer 362 (Cowal West & Isle of Bute)

This delightful walk starts near the remains of Glendaruel House, a Scots Baronial Mansion that was the seat of the Campbells of Glendaruel until 1900. It was modernized by Lewis Wiggan, a wealthy businessman, then sold to Harrisson Cripps who was the King's surgeon. Just before the Second World War Cripps' nephew, Sir Stafford Cripps, then Chancellor of the Exchequer entertained the German Chancellor here. Glendaruel was a hospital during the war years and was then sold off as a hotel. It was destroyed by fire in 1970.

From the car park follow the road towards the site reception. Pass this to the left to reach a T-junction **Ⓐ**. Turn left along a narrow road and proceed to a public bridleway sign to the main road. On your left are three gothic stone arches – all that remain of the Lucknow Gates, the original entrance to Glendaruel Estate. According to local lore the gates were named to commemorate the relief of the Siege of Lucknow by General Sir Colin Campbell.

Ignore the turning onto the bridleway and continue along the narrow road. This road is shown on George Langland's Map of Argyll, 1801, and is probably the oldest road through the glen. It runs through Clachan of Glendaruel to Dounans (Dunans).

Keep on the road for 1½ miles (2.4km) then cross an old stone bridge, pass a children's play area on the right before turning right onto a path **Ⓑ** then right again at the main road into the village.

Continue through the village to reach

Kilmodan church at Glendaruel

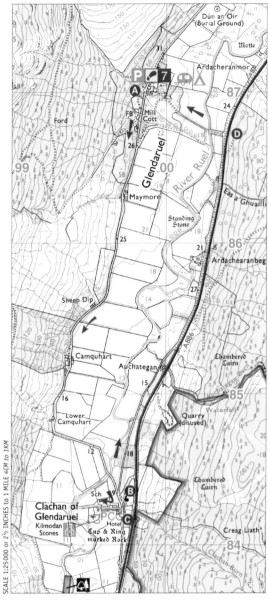

SCALE 1:25000 or 2½ INCHES to 1 MILE 4CM to 1KM

look closely you will see that it once had three entrances. Locals will tell you that this was for the three Campbell lairds who worshipped here. Although related they were not on speaking terms and refused to enter the church by the same door. The 17th-century stone on one of the exterior walls is said to commemorate Sir Dugald Campbell of Auchenbreck.

The old burial enclosure in the far corner of the churchyard is thought to have been that of the Campbells of Auchenbreck. Now it houses a selection of the richly carved stones that Kilmodan is noted for. Included here are some examples of the work of the school of carvers that was centred in the Loch Awe area in the 14th and 15th centuries. Retrace your steps to **B** then turn right onto a narrow lane. Follow it past two houses to reach a T-junction with the main road. Immediately before the road turn left onto a track. This is part of the old road through the Glen and runs parallel with the main road. Follow it to eventually reach the entrance to a bungalow. Keep straight ahead here along a muddy tree-lined track. When you exit the trees beside another bungalow keep ahead on a narrow lane, then turn right at the drive for Glendaruel Caravan Park **D** then follow it to the start of the walk. ●

a telephone box **C**, then turn right along a lane and turning left where the lane forks at the entrance to Kilmodan School to reach the churchyard.

The parish of Kilmodan first appears in ecclesiastical records in 1250 and the present church which dates from 1783 is the third to be built on this site. If you

Tobermory and Aros Park

Start	Tobermory, Ledaig car park at south end of harbour
Distance	4½ miles (7.2km)
Approximate time	2½ hours
Parking	Tobermory
Refreshments	Pubs and cafés at Tobermory
Ordnance Survey maps	Landranger 47 (Tobermory & North Mull), Explorer 374 (Isle of Mull North & Tobermory)

An attractive, wooded path along the side of Tobermory Bay leads to Aros Park, the former estate of the now demolished Aros House, renowned for its fine collection of rhododendrons and its woodland, waterfalls and lochan. After a circuit of the park, you retrace your steps to Tobermory. There is plenty of variety for a relatively short walk, and a series of grand views across the bay.

Tobermory was founded in 1788 as a fishing village by the British Fisheries Society. The mixture of grey stone and brightly painted buildings along the curving waterfront and its particularly fine sheltered harbour – usually full of fishing vessels, yachts and all kinds of pleasure boats – gives it a most attractive and in fine weather even

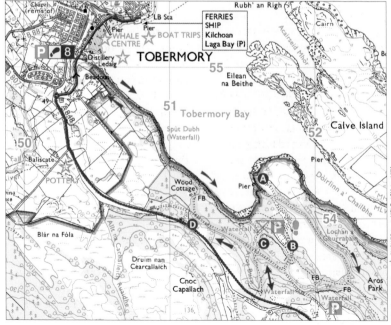

Colourful Tobermory

Mediterranean appearance. The wreck of a Spanish galleon in the bay, long thought to have been a treasure ship, has now been confirmed as one of the Armada fleet which was destroyed by a powder explosion after putting into the harbour for repairs in November 1588.

A path, signposted 'Forest Walk', leads off from the far end of the car park and climbs gently through woodland along the side of Tobermory Bay, following a red-waymarked route. The views through the trees to the left across the bay are superb.

On reaching a barrier there is, at the time of writing, a diversion. Turn right and then bear left – the new path is above the old one – and look out for where the path turns sharp left and zigzags steeply downhill to rejoin the original route. Keep ahead to cross a footbridge over a burn by the Lower Falls, at a fork take the left-hand path – the 'Pier Path' – and descend to cross another footbridge over a burn in front of a building, Mill Cottage **Ⓐ**.

Turn left to the pier for a grand view of Tobermory across the bay; otherwise the route continues to the right along a track to Lochan a Ghurrabain. Turn first left and then right to walk along the very attractive, tree-lined 'Loch Path', with the lochan on the right, and follow it around the far end of the lochan to a fork. Take the blue-waymarked right-hand path which curves right, keeps along the other side of the lochan and, after crossing a footbridge over a burn, brings you to a T-junction.

Turn left on to a yellow-waymarked path which winds steeply uphill and bends right to continue above the lochan. At a crossroads turn left along a track **Ⓑ** – soon it becomes a tarmac track – which curves right.

At a bridge **Ⓒ** you can make a brief detour to the left on to a path signposted 'Upper Falls' and head steeply uphill to view this impressive sight. Return to the tarmac track **Ⓒ**, turn left over the bridge and, after just over $\frac{1}{4}$ mile (400m), look out for a yellow-topped post where you bear right downhill along a rough track **Ⓓ**.

At a white cottage turn right on to a path to enter trees, by a sign to Tobermory, and descend some steps to join the outward route by the start of the diversion. From here retrace your steps to the start. ●

Campbeltown Loch

Start	Campbeltown
Distance	4½ miles (7.2km)
Approximate time	2 hours
Parking	Campbeltown
Refreshments	Pubs and cafés at Campbeltown
Ordnance Survey maps	Landranger 68 (South Kintyre & Campbeltown), Explorer 356 (Kintyre South)

From the harbour at Campbeltown the forested slopes of Beinn Ghuilean can be seen rising above the town to the south. The route begins by heading out of the town and continues across fields above Crosshill Loch to the edge of the forest. Then follows a short loop through the forest, climbing up above the trees on to open moorland. From the higher points the views across Campbeltown Loch and Kintyre are both extensive and superb.

Campbeltown is by far the largest town in Kintyre and lies around its fishing harbour at the head of Campbeltown Loch. It has long been famed for its whisky distilleries; in Victorian times there were over 30 of these and it was said that sea captains could find their way into the harbour simply by using their sense of smell.

🥾 The walk begins by the harbour in front of the tourist information centre. Walk along Main Street, turn right into Lorne Street, following signs to Machrihanish and Southend, continue along Witchburn Road and take the first turning on the left **Ⓐ** after

Campbeltown Loch

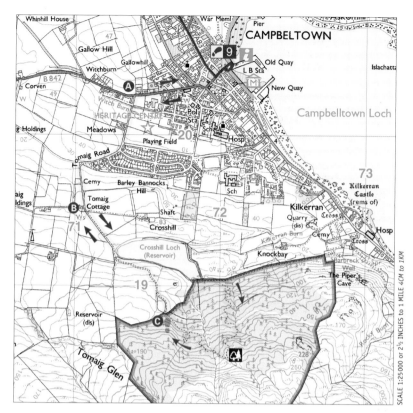

passing the Campbeltown Creamery. The road – Tomaig Road – bends right through a new housing area, then bends left and heads uphill.

Where it bends right again **B**, keep ahead along a track and climb a stile at a left bend. Continue along the track ahead towards the forested slopes of Beinn Ghuilean, go through a kissing-gate and pass the end of Crosshill Loch. After climbing a stile, the track bears left uphill above the loch and winds up to a kissing-gate on the edge of the forest **C**.

Go through the gate and in front of a Forest Enterprise board turn left to follow a circular, waymarked trail, looking out for the regular blue footprints. At first head downhill through the conifers, going round a number of bends and crossing several footbridges, to the corner of Crosshill Loch. Keep ahead, turn right up steps at a blue waymark and the route continues

uphill, quite steeply at times, around more sharp bends and up a long flight of steps, to emerge from the trees into more open country.

Continue climbing across bracken- and heather-covered slopes, first to a picnic table and then on to a bench. This is the highest point on the walk and the best of a series of magnificent viewpoints over Crosshill Loch, Campbeltown and its loch, the mountains of Arran and both the east and west coasts of Kintyre, with the Atlantic breakers rolling in on the west.

The path now curves right and descends into the conifers again, via more steps, bends and footbridges, to the kissing-gate on the edge of the forest **C**. Go through, here rejoining the outward route, and retrace your steps to the start at Campbeltown. ●

Salen

Start	Salen
Distance	4 miles (6.4km)
Approximate time	2 hours
Parking	Roadside parking at Salen
Refreshments	Hotel and café at Salen
Ordnance Survey maps	Landranger 47 (Tobermory & North Mull), Explorer 374 (Isle of Mull North & Tobermory)

An initial gentle climb along a clear path, through woodland and across fields, is followed by rougher walking across grassy moorland, from which there are impressive views of the Ben More group and Loch na Keal. On the return path come more fine views, this time looking across the Sound of Mull to the mainland. There is some rough walking and overgrown paths in places and the route directions between Ⓑ and Ⓒ need to be followed carefully.

Woodland near Salen

The walk begins at the road junction by the church in the pleasant village of Salen. Take the Tobermory road and after just over ¼ mile (400m), bear left Ⓐ through a metal kissing-gate and walk along an attractive, wooded, gently ascending path. There are superb views through the trees on the right across the Sound of Mull.

As the path continues through a succession of metal gates, initially by a wall bordering woodland on the left and later by a wire fence, the ruins of the medieval Aros Castle can be seen over to the right, one of a chain of powerful fortresses guarding the Sound of Mull. Eventually you reach a stile just to the left of the farm buildings surrounding Glenaros House **B**. Climb it, keep ahead towards a cottage, go through two metal gates in quick succession – there is a sign 'Path to Loch na Keal via Fort' – and continue along a track which curves left and heads gently uphill across rough, grassy moorland, by a wall on the left.

Ahead is a hill crowned by the remains of the fort of Cnoc na Sròine. Keep ahead towards it after the wall on the left ends, and at a fork take the left-hand track which curves slightly left towards the fort. Bear right to ford a burn (Allt a' Chaisteil) and continue along the track, which climbs to a pass to the right of the hillfort. You can make a brief detour to the left to inspect the walls of the fort and take in the superb view from the top.

From the top of the pass there is a very good view ahead of the Ben More group of peaks and, as you gently descend, Loch na Keal comes into sight. The track narrows to a path, becomes less and less distinct and finally peters out altogether.

Continue downhill across rough grass and ford a burn, then keep ahead

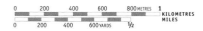

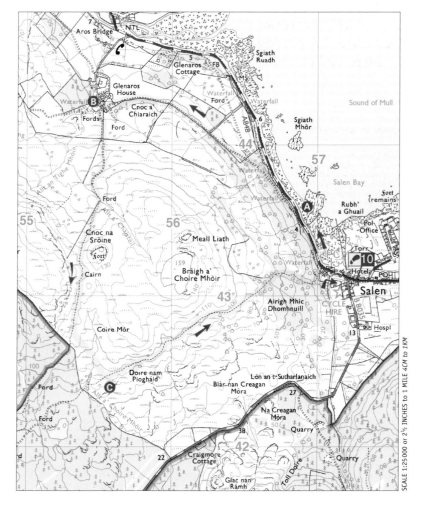

parallel to the burn, making for the edge of a conifer plantation.

On reaching a clear and definite path , turn left and follow it through trees, grass and bracken. At times the path is narrow, boggy, indistinct and engulfed by bracken, but it improves as you climb gently over the shoulder of a hill. Now there are fine views ahead across the Sound of Mull to the mainland, and as you descend, Salen comes into sight. The path enters woodland and heads down to a stile. Climb it, continue winding downhill through this most attractive woodland, finally descending to a track on the edge of Salen. Turn left to a road and turn right back to the village centre.

Looking south from the fort of Cnoc na Sròine

Isle of Lismore

Start	Achnacroish
Distance	4½ miles (7.2km)
Approximate time	2½ hours
Parking	Oban, near the ferry terminal
Refreshments	None
Ordnance Survey maps	Landranger 49 (Oban & East Mull), Explorer 376 (Oban & North Lorn)

Lismore is a long, low, narrow island in the middle of Loch Linnhe, reached by a regular ferry service from Oban. Its narrowness and flatness give it two great advantages for walkers, especially for those not looking for anything too strenuous: the walking is relatively easy and relaxing, and the glorious views across to the West Highlands and mountains of Mull are unimpeded. Historic interest is provided by the former cathedral of the bishops of Argyll and the broch at Tirefour. Note that the ferry service from Oban to Lismore does not operate on Sundays.

From the pier at Achnacroish, walk up the road and at a public footpath sign to Balnagown, turn right along a track that passes in front of cottages. Go through a metal gate, pass in front of some more cottages and bear right to a metal kissing-gate.

Go through and continue along the coast path – which may be wet and muddy in places – beneath low cliffs. Go through another metal kissing-gate by a monument to a man who was drowned off this spot when his sailing boat went down in 1891. Descend to cross a footbridge over a small burn, keep ahead to go through a metal gate to the left of a cottage and bear left gently uphill to a footpath post in front of a house **A**.

Bear left through a gate, keep ahead along a tarmac drive, passing to the left of Loch Baile a' Ghobhainn, go through a metal gate and continue up to reach the island's narrow road **B**. Just to the left of this junction is Lismore Historical Society's award-winning construction of a croft house. This is open each day in the summer season with the exception of Wednesday. Hours are 11.00 – 16.00. Turn right and after ½ mile (800m) you reach Clachan. The small whitewashed church is the reconstituted choir of the cathedral of the medieval bishops of Argyll, completed in the 14th century. St Moluag, a contemporary of St Columba, arrived on Lismore in the 6th century and made the island, like Iona, a centre for teaching and evangelical work. There is no trace of the earliest Christian buildings on the island. The nave and tower of the cathedral were destroyed after the Reformation and the choir fell into ruin before being restored in the 18th century to serve as the parish church.

View of the mainland from Lismore

Some of the foundations of the medieval cathedral can be seen to the west of the church.

Continue along the road and soon you pass a pile of rocks called Moluag's Chair, a fine viewpoint where, according to tradition, the saint used to sit and meditate. From now on the views, both ahead and on either side across to the mountains on the mainland, are magnificent.

At a sign 'Balure and Broch' turn sharp right ⊙, go through a metal gate and walk along a tarmac track, bearing right by a farm and passing through two more metal gates.

Over to the left is Tirefour Castle, a Pictish broch probably constructed sometime after 500 BC. A gate on the left gives access, and from here there

are more spectacular views – on a clear day extending to Ben Nevis, Ben Cruachan and even the Paps of Jura.

Continue along the track, bending right towards another farm and then turning left to go through a metal gate, at a public footpath sign to Balnagown. Now the track becomes a rough one, likely to be muddy in places, which continues across a meadow. Pass to the left of an abandoned cottage, head gently uphill between gorse bushes and then descend and bear right to go through a gate beside Loch Baile a' Ghobhainn. Walk beside the loch, later keep along the right edge of a meadow, joining a wall on the right, and go through a metal gate in the far corner. Continue by a burn, turn right to cross it and head up to a tarmac drive. Turn left, here rejoining the outward route, and retrace your steps to the start. ●

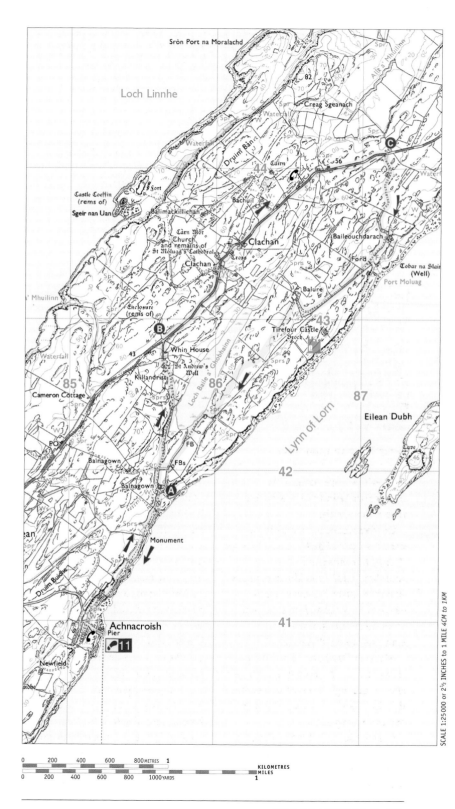

Loch Linnhe

Sròn Port na Moralachd

Creag Sgeanach

C

82

44 Cairn

Druim Bàn

Bachuil

Castle Coeffin (rems of)

Sgeir nan Uan

Sort

Balimackillichan

Càrn Mòr Church and remains of St Moluag's Cathedral

Clachan

Cross

Clachan

Baileouchdarach

Ford

Tobar na Slair (Well)

Port Moluag

Balure

' Mhuilinn

Enclosure (rems of)

B

Whin House

Tirefour Castle Broch

43

St Andrew's Well

86

87

Eilean Dubh

Killandrist

Loch Baile a' Ghobhainn

Cameron Cottage

85

43

POT

Lynn of Lorn

42

Cave 46

Balnagown

FB

Balnagown

FBs

A

Monument

41

ean

Druim Buidhe

Achnacroish
Pier

11

Newfield

SCALE 1:25 000 or 2½ INCHES to 1 MILE 4CM to 1KM

0   200   400   600   800 METRES   1

0   200   400   600   800   1000 YARDS   1

KILOMETRES

MILES

1

Loch Avich

Start	Dalavich, on the north-west shore of Loch Awe
Distance	5 miles (8km)
Approximate time	2½ hours
Parking	Forestry Commission picnic site at Barnaline, Dalavich
Refreshments	Tearoom at Inverinan, 3 miles (4.8km) north-east of Dalavich
Ordnance Survey maps	Landranger 55 (Lochgilphead & Loch Awe), Explorer 360 (Loch Awe & Inveraray)

The Forestry Commission have gone to great trouble and expense to attract the public to their walks from Dalavich and Inverinan. Each of these walks has its own appeal: the Loch Avich route featured here is one of the most strenuous, following a tortuous switchback route to the unfrequented south shore of the loch before returning via the path following the River Avich. Although the path has been greatly improved recently, it can still be muddy in places.

From the car park follow the yellow footpath signs for the Loch Avich Walk. This will take you through the Dalavich Oakwood, an important preserve of the broadleafed woodland which once covered much of the hillside here. Go through a gate then turn right at a T-junction **A** and head uphill to the visitor centre in a former stable. This is all that remains of Barnaline Farm. Inside, the horse stalls remain and there is a display of harness and agricultural implements. Several interpretation boards provide information on the history of the area and the

animals, birds and insects that make their homes in the surrounding woodland.

Continue uphill from the centre, passing some ruined buildings then turn right at a junction beside a sheep fank. Go through a gate in the deer fence and follow the road as it curves left to join the forest road at a yellow footprint marker. The forest road continues on a level course for another ½ mile (800m) until, about 1½ miles (2.4km) after the start, it bears to the left and descends. Follow the footprint symbol to the right here **B** on to a lesser, embanked track which follows the uneven ground like a big dipper and makes exhilarating walking.

The path soon comes to a remarkable natural amphitheatre known as the 'Dry Loch' **C**. Beyond this there are some crumbling stone walls which once belonged to the fields and houses of old crofts. Trees flourish on this land, which was under cultivation two centuries ago. From here to Loch Avich a wide variety of coniferous species have been planted and some stray broadleaved trees have also become established.

The 'Dry Loch'

Look out for the rare and distinctive Japanese cedar (*Cryptomeria*), an experimental planting of the 1950s.

The path descends quite steeply to reach the shore of Loch Avich by a fishing hut **D**.

It takes about an hour to reach this point, the start of a delightful section of the route close to the shore of the loch. The trees here are oak, ash and birch, which provide a colourful foreground in spring and autumn. There is an imposing hunting lodge on the other side of the loch (Lochavich House). The path continues to pursue its switchback style and it seems no time before the bank of the River Avich is reached **E**.

The path now follows the river downstream through woodland which is quite dense at times. The waterfall is heard but never seen (though easily visited by using another forestry trail). When the original forest road is reached turn left to return to the car park. ●

Dùn na Cuaiche, Inveraray

Start	Inveraray Castle
Distance	2½ miles (4km)
Approximate time	2 hours
Parking	Inveraray Castle
Refreshments	Tearoom at castle
Ordnance Survey maps	Landranger 56 (Loch Lomond & Inveraray), Explorers 360 (Loch Awe & Inverary) and 363 (Cowal East)

Dùn na Cuaiche was strategically important to the Campbells, who could watch the mouths of three glens from the summit – Glen Fyne, Glen Aray and Glen Shira. Long before the coming of the Campbells, however, earlier settlers had recognised the height's defensive potential: there are remains of what may be Iron Age ramparts on the summit. In 1748 William Adam and Roger Morris erected the folly tower on Dùn na Cuaiche which adds to its picturesque appeal. The reward for the short climb (which is not for the faint-hearted or those not used to exercise) is a remarkable vista over Inveraray town and castle to mountains far distant.

Head north from the car park (the forecourt of the castle) past the monument which commemorates the execution of 17 Clan Campbell leaders by the first Marquis of Atholl in Inveraray in 1685. Cross the bridge and ignore the first track on the right but immediately after it turn right onto a path through the woods **A** marked by blue and red waymarkers. This lovely shady path emerges from the woods, via a kissing-gate, then crosses a track and a field to reach a green gate (fasten this behind you). This leads into the arboretum which contains a host of specimen trees, many of them dating from the reign of Queen Victoria; some are even older.

The path now climbs past old kilns; these were built to provide lime to make the peaty soil of the Highlands less acidic and thus more fertile. Ignore the yellow waymarker on the right and continue to the next turn which is marked by a blue waymarker **B**. Turn right here then sharp left to head uphill on a narrow path. When it joins a wider path turn right and continue along it to the next blue marker. Turn left up a set of steps here. The going is steep and the path narrow, often with a rope on the right-hand side to prevent unpleasant falls down precipitous slopes should one slip. *Keep a careful watch on children here.*

A grand view is revealed as the path skirts a scree slope along a narrow ledge. Soon after this the narrow path joins with a wider one which continues to zigzag upwards, though in rather less spectacular style. There are now views to the north-west up Glen Aray. The

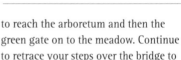

folly tower **C** is revealed at the last moment. The views from here are truly magnificent and the exhausting climb is soon forgotten as one appreciates the scenery from this vantage point.

To return to the castle, retrace your steps down the carriageway to the point where it was joined by the footpath on the way up. However, do not turn right here but continue on the main track which twists down the hill on a comparatively gentle gradient. After passing Point 6 on the left **B** carry on

Inveraray town and castle from Dùn na Cuaiche

to reach the arboretum and then the green gate on to the meadow. Continue to retrace your steps over the bridge to the castle, where refreshments are available from the tearoom in the holiday season.

Alternative routes are offered in the excellent leaflet on the Dùn na Cuaiche Woodland Walks; this is obtainable from the castle kiosk when the castle is open, or at other times from the Estate Office or Tourist Information Centre. ●

Beinn Lora

Start	Benderloch
Distance	4 miles (6.4km)
Approximate time	2 hours
Parking	Benderloch, either the Forestry Commission Beinn Lora car park or the larger one on the opposite side of the road
Refreshments	Café at Benderloch
Ordnance Survey maps	Landranger 49 (Oban & East Mull), Explorer 376 (Oban & North Lorn)

Although only a short walk that takes you to the relatively modest height of 1010ft (308m), the climb up to the summit of Beinn Lora is quite steep in parts. The lower part of the route is through woodland, passing a succession of outstanding viewpoints both on the way up and on the descent, and the finest views of all come when you emerge on to open moorland just below the summit. The whole of the walk is on clear and well-waymarked forest paths.

From the Forestry Commission car park take the path that leads into the trees and, at an information board, bear left, go through a kissing-gate and then follow the path to the left. The first part of the route follows blue- and red-topped posts. Climb steadily, initially

through broadleaved woodland, and after a right-hand bend the path ascends more steeply through conifers. At the point where the red- and blue-

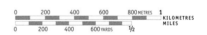

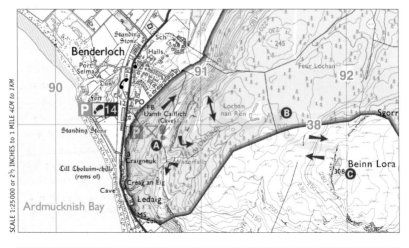

View from the slopes of Beinn Lora

waymarked route turns right to a viewpoint **A**, keep ahead uphill, now following blue-topped posts only.

At a fork take the left-hand path, signposted to Eagles Eyrie Viewpoint, for a brief detour to enjoy the superb views northwards up Loch Linnhe towards Ben Nevis and eastwards across the loch to the isle of Lismore and the mountains of Morvern.

Return to the fork, turn left, in the Beinn Lora direction, and continue steadily uphill. The path bends right and heads up to a gate on the edge of the forest **B**. This is another fine viewpoint, this time looking southwards towards Loch Etive and Oban. Go through the gate and follow a path across grassy and heathery moorland to the flat summit of Beinn Lora. Initially the path descends slightly before a short but steep pull leads up to the triangulation pillar **C**. The wonderful views from here – northwards to Loch Linnhe, Loch Creran and Ben Nevis; eastwards to Loch Etive and Ben Cruachan; southwards to Oban and the Isle of Kerrera; and westwards to Morvern and the isles of Mull and Lismore – totally dispel the myth that you have to scale great heights and conquer mighty peaks in order to reach the best viewpoints. There can be few finer sights in the whole of the Western Highlands, and a short walk to the end of the summit ridge brings Connel and the flat country of the Moss of Achnacree, with its small lochs, into view below.

Retrace your steps to where you left the red- and blue-waymarked route and turn left **A** to enjoy another superb viewpoint. Turn left again along a path that runs initially parallel to and below the previous path, following it steadily downhill and curving gradually right all the while. At a fork take the left-hand path which descends quite steeply to a T-junction. Turn left and retrace your steps to the start.

Connel and the Black Lochs

Start	Connel
Distance	5½ miles (8.9km)
Approximate time	3 hours
Parking	Connel, station car park
Refreshments	Hotels at Connel
Ordnance Survey maps	Landranger 49 (Oban & East Mull), Explorers 376 (Oban & North Lorn) and 359 (Oban, Kerrera & Loch Melfort)

From the village of Connel, situated at the mouth of Loch Etive, the route first follows a quiet lane through the valley of the Lusragan Burn and then continues along clear tracks, passing by the group of remote and mysterious-looking Black Lochs of Kilvaree. There are fine views throughout, with Ben Cruachan in sight for part of the way, and on the final leg come particularly outstanding views over Connel, Loch Etive and the Lynn of Lorn.

Connel is situated on the southern shores of Loch Etive where a bridge carries the main road between Oban and Fort William over the mouth of the loch.

Start in the centre of the village by the bridge over Lusragan Burn and take the path beside the burn, passing under the railway viaduct. Go through a metal gate, then head gently uphill, passing to the left of a house, and continue to a lane **A**.

Bear left along this narrow lane through the valley of Lusragan Burn, passing to the left of an ancient hillfort, and after two miles (3.2km) – just before the top of a slight rise – turn left on to a track **B** and go through a metal gate. The track winds downhill and crosses a bridge over the burn.

Follow the clear, well-surfaced, winding track across open country to Lower Loch, the first of the Black Lochs, whose marshy and reedy banks almost entirely obliterate the water. The track keeps alongside the loch before

ascending and continuing above – and some distance from – Middle Loch, heading towards Kilvaree Farm. Do not go through the metal gate before the farm but keep ahead by a wall and wire fence on the right. Where the wall turns right, bear right and walk across a field corner to join and keep by a wire fence on the right. At the fence corner bear right again and head across rough and boggy ground, by ruined buildings, to a metal gate **C**.

Go through the gate and keep along a grassy track above Middle Loch, a very attractive part of the walk with Ben Cruachan dominating the scene. Go through another gate and continue above Upper Loch – the path climbs and bears left away from the water, keeping below slopes on the left.

After bearing right to go through a metal gate, you go across undulating

0	200	400	600	800 METRES	1	
						KILOMETRES
						MILES
0	200	400	600 YARDS	½		

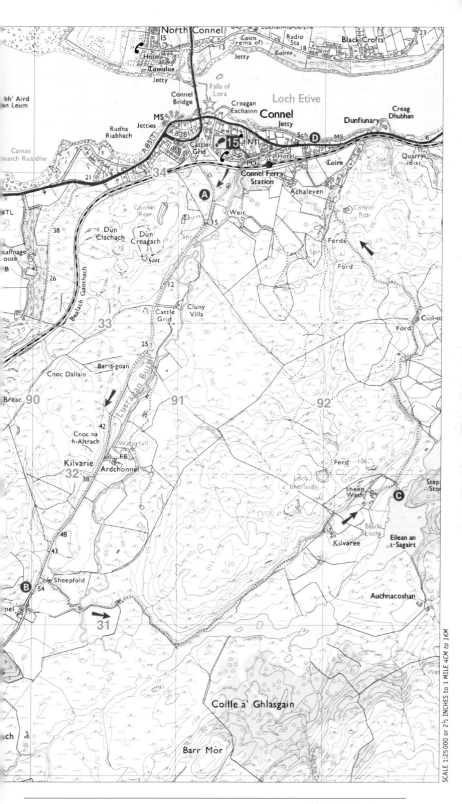

SCALE 1:25000 or 2½ INCHES to 1 MILE 4CM to 1KM

heathery moorland, passing a rather precarious-looking large boulder on a small hill to the left and the meagre ruins of Cuil-uaine, once a reasonably large settlement. Soon superb views open up ahead over Loch Etive and the Lynn of Lorn to the majestic hills beyond, with Connel and its bridge in the foreground. Descend to a metal gate, go through the gate and continue down to Achaleven Farm. Pass to the left of the farm and keep ahead along a tarmac track which curves right and passes under a railway bridge to a main road **Ⓓ**.

Turn left into Connel and take the first turning on the left, signposted 'Village', to return to the start. ●

The Black Lochs of Kilvaree

Isle of Kerrera

Start	Kerrera Jetty
Distance	6 miles (9.7km)
Approximate time	3½ hours
Parking	Kerrera Ferry slipway, Gallanach road, 2 miles (3.2km) south-west of Oban
Refreshments	Kerrera Tea Garden
Ordnance Survey maps	Landranger 49 (Oban & East Mull), Explorers 359 (Oban, Kerrera & Loch Melfort) and 376 (Oban & North Lorn)

The earliest ferry to the isle of Kerrera departs at 08.45am in season and the next is at 10.30am. Thereafter there is a regular service (every hour or so), with intending passengers being asked to turn a board to show the ferryman that he is in fact wanted at the advertised times (in any event it would be as well to check with Oban Tourist Information Centre first – see the list of useful organisations on pages 94 and 95). Kerrera has the air of romance about it common to all the islands off this coast. It is an intensely beautiful place, well worth the small effort involved in getting there.

On landing turn left at the telephone box along the track which follows the eastern shore of the island. There are lovely coastal views across the Horse Shoe to the Sound of Kerrera and the mainland beyond. The track goes through a gate before the first farm (Ardchoirc): fork left here to continue along the coast. The field on the left is called Dail Righ, the 'King's Field', where Alexander II of Scotland died in 1249. The crofts of Gallanach are well seen on the other side of the Sound, below steep crags, while Oban is to the north-east.

The Little Horse Shoe is a tiny bay which appears to be a graveyard of fishing boats. The track passes in front of the lovely whitewashed cottages overlooking the bay, which is sheltered by a steep, tree-covered hill. The track continues, snaking uphill to lose the view of the sea, though mainland peaks are just visible to the south-east.

Fork to the right Ⓐ just before the white cottage of Upper Gylen. Continue on this track to reach another white cottage, this time Lower Gylen. This now operates in the summer months as the Kerrera Tea Garden. Here you can taste some superb home-made soups and home-baking. Retrace your steps from the cottage and turn right through a gate signed for Gylen Castle and follow the footpath to reach the ruins Ⓑ. The castle had a short history, being built in 1582 by the MacDougalls of Dunollie and lasting only until 1647 when it was left a ruin by Covenanters.

From the castle follow the cliffs west, crossing a stream and taking a path at

SCALE 1:25000 or 2½ INCHES to 1 MILE 4CM to 1KM

0	200	400	600	800 METRES	1
					KILOMETRES
					MILES
0	200	400	600 YARDS	½	

the foot of a steep crag to turn north. This path joins a track **C** on to which you turn left to pass two cottages, the second one (Ardmore) derelict. The narrow path which is followed uphill from the remains of the second cottage was once a drove road. Cattle from Mull were landed on Kerrera at Barr-nam-boc Bay and driven south to be shipped to the mainland from the tiny haven of Port Dubh. (Alternatively they would be swum to the mainland from the east coast of the island.)

Level ground is soon reached above Ardmore and the views to Mull and Lismore improve as the path heads northwards. Morvern lies beyond the lighthouse on Lismore.

The going is easy on this smooth grassy path, which descends to another deserted croft – Barnabuck **D**. Presumably it is the shelter offered by Mull which allows trees to grow in this enchantingly beautiful spot.

Take the zigzag track up the hill from Barnabuck. There is a fine view when the crest of the hill is reached, and Oban will soon be seen ahead, with the distinctive shape of Ben Cruachan in the distance (on a clear day you will see Ben Nevis too). When the track meets with the one from Slaterich turn right to return to the ferry. ●

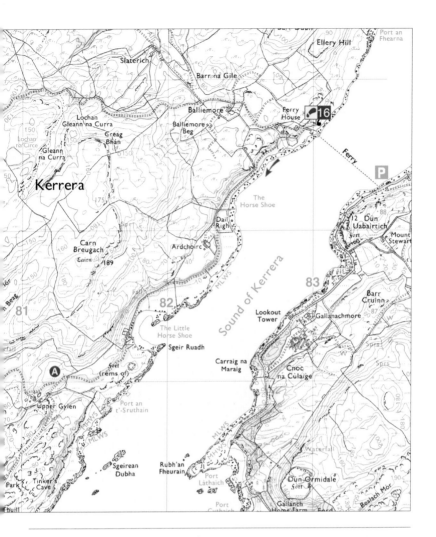

The Sound of Kerrera from The Little Horse Shoe

Garmony Point and the Fishnish Peninsula

Start	Forestry Commission's Garmony car park, off A849, 4 miles (6.4km) north of the Craignure ferry terminal
Distance	7 miles (11.3km)
Approximate time	3 hours
Parking	Garmony car park
Refreshments	Kiosk at Fishnish ferry terminal
Ordnance Survey maps	Landranger 49 (Oban & East Mull), Explorer 375 (Isle of Mull East)

After an initial walk across coastal marshes, parts of which may be wet and soft, the remainder of this well-waymarked route is through the conifer woodlands of the Fishnish Peninsula on the east coast of Mull. There are fine views across the Sound of Mull to Loch Aline and the cliffs and hills of Morvern on the mainland.

From the car park there is immediately a grand view across Garmony Point of the cliffs of Morvern on the opposite side of the Sound of Mull.

🖉 Begin by turning left, at a foot-path post marked 'Garmony to Fishnish', and follow a winding path across the marshland fringing the coast, looking

The cliffs of Morvern from Garmony Point

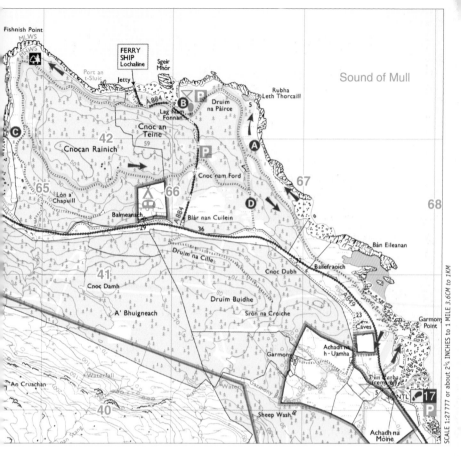

out for the regular red-waymarked posts. The path, narrow in places but generally clear, eventually reaches a gate.

Go through the gate, keep ahead between rough grass, bracken and young conifers, and the path winds round to a T-junction **A**.

Turn right along a track, now following green waymarks for most of the rest of the walk. The track keeps alongside the shore, turning left and passing beside a metal barrier to join another track at a bend. Keep ahead, at a T-junction turn right **B** along a road and where the road bends right to Fishnish ferry terminal, keep ahead along an ascending track to enter conifer woodland.

Go through a gate and continue to the fine viewpoint of Fishnish Point, where the track curves left to run parallel

to the western shore. In the past the Fishnish Peninsula was well populated, with four villages and a harbour from which cattle were shipped across the Sound of Mull. Some of the ruined buildings can be seen.

At a fork take the left-hand track **C**, still following green waymarks, and after going through another gate the track emerges into more open country, bending first left and then right to reach a road.

Cross the road, turn first left and then right and continue to a T-junction. Turn left **D** and at a red-waymarked post, turn right on to a path **A**, here picking up the outward route, and retrace your steps to the start. ●

Ardcastle Wood

Start	Ardcastle Wood, 2 miles (3.25km) north of Lochgair on the north-west shore of Loch Fyne
Distance	5 miles (8km)
Approximate time	3 hours
Parking	Forestry picnic area off A83 2 miles (3.2km) north of Lochgair
Refreshments	Hotel at Lochgair
Ordnance Survey maps	Landranger 55 (Lochgilphead & Loch Awe), Explorer 362 (Cowal West & Isle of Bute)

This must be one of the very best of all Forestry Commission walks. Forestry tracks are used for some of the way but they never seem tedious and the pines are particularly fragrant. The main feature of the route is the long stretch beside a seldom-visited part of the Loch Fyne shoreline. Wildlife abounds here – you will see a range of birds from goldcrests to waders, and might even encounter an otter. As you will see from the Forestry map at the start of the walk, the blue and white routes are shortcuts; however, the odds are that you will not be inclined to use them.

There is a good viewpoint at the car park, overlooking Loch Gair and Loch Fyne.

✎ Leave the car park turn right and go through a gate onto a forest road. After approximately 109 yds (100m) turn left onto a grass track following the yellow footprint markers. The fine hills on the left surround Loch Dubh to the east of Loch Glashan. At the T-junction with the forest road turn left. The red route leaves to the right **A** to climb to a viewpoint, and soon afterwards the route described here also branches right on to a grassy track which wends its way down to the lochside, following the right bank of a burn which reaches the shore by flowing down a small waterfall on to the beach **B**.

It only takes 20 minutes to reach this beauty-spot, ideal for a picnic overlooking the loch. The path south follows close to the shore, birches, foxgloves and yellow irises providing foregrounds for panoramas of water and mountain. When the path joins with a track, walking remains a pleasure, the pines being exceptionally resinous. A small bay is skirted before the blue route, the first Forestry Commission shortcut, leaves inland **C**. The track enters tall stands of timber which screen views of Loch Fyne, and a minor track branches to the left **D** to another picnic place sited on a rocky promontory overlooking a beach.

From the picnic place walk down to the sand quarry which is a habitat of shy common lizards (and possibly snakes as well).

Another forest track is reached on the other side of the quarry, and as this begins to climb, a junction is reached where a right turn will lead you on a shortcut back to the car park. **E** Turn left and continue climbing; there is a pair of well-sited seats at the top and fine views up and down the loch. A grassy path descends to an old quarry and then rounds Rubha na Drochaid to reach another picnic place **F**. The

writer has watched otters from here as they scrambled over rocks and swam in Loch Gair, a lagoon which looks as though it belongs to the South Seas rather than the Highlands.

The path now rejoins a forest track to

begin the return. Abundant thistles here provide goldcrests with a feast of seeds and they will feed greedily as people walk by. Look for a mown path on the left which goes to St Bride's graveyard and ruined chapel Ⓖ – a lovely place to rest, briefly or eternally. Leave the forest track at a yellow waymarker on the right onto a path through woodlands. At a T-junction turn right and continue on the path along the edge of the forest. At a deer fence go through a kissing-gate and a short distance farther on through another kissing-gate to rejoin the forest track. Turn left at the next yellow waymarker onto a path leading back to the car park. ●

Loch Fyne from Ardcastle Wood

Port Askaig and Ballygrant

Start	Port Askaig
Distance	7½ miles (12.1km)
Approximate time	3½ hours
Parking	Port Askaig
Refreshments	Hotel at Port Askaig, hotel at Ballygrant
Ordnance Survey maps	Landrangers 60 (Islay) and 61 (Jura & Colonsay), Explorers 353 (Islay North) and 355 (Jura & Scarba)

There are fine views across both Islay and Jura from this walk on the east side of Islay. After a short coastal stretch above the Sound of Islay to the distillery at Caol Ila, the route continues along the road into Ballygrant. The return to Port Askaig follows a clear track through delightful woodland and beside lochs. If you wish to avoid the road walking, you could take a bus – there is a fairly frequent service – from Port Askaig to Ballygrant and start the walk from point **C**.

Port Askaig comprises very little more than a hotel and shop. From Port Askaig there are ferries to the mainland and across the narrow Sound of Islay to the isle of Jura.

Begin by heading steeply uphill along the road, follow the road around a right bend and, at a sharp left bend, go through a metal gate **A**. Continue along a path which climbs between trees and bracken and keeps above the coast, with superb views to the right across the Sound of Islay to the barren wastes of Jura and the distinctive peaks of the Paps of Jura. The undulating path – likely to be overgrown by bracken in places – heads towards the distillery at Caol Ila and bears left alongside a wire fence on the right. At a fence corner turn right over a stile and descend to a lane by the distillery.

Turn left along the lane, which curves left and then continues up to rejoin the road **B**. Turn right and walk along it to

Beautiful Lily Loch

Loch Ballygrant

Ballygrant, a distance of just over
2$\frac{1}{2}$ miles (4km). After about $\frac{1}{2}$ mile
(800m), you pass through the village of
Keills where a brief detour to the right
brings you to the scanty remains of a
medieval chapel.

At Ballygrant turn left along a lane
signposted to Mulindry **C**, take the
left-hand lane at a fork **D** and after
100 yds (91m), turn left through a metal
gate. Walk along a woodland track and
turn left at a T-junction to continue
beside the wooded shores of Loch
Ballygrant. This is a most attractive part
of the walk with delightful views across
the loch.

After the track leaves the loch, the
route continues either through or along
the edge of more woodland, later
keeping along the shore of the
appropriately named Lily Loch. Curve
right around the end of the loch, head
uphill – there are very good views to the
right from here across the loch – and
then curve left to continue up to a metal
gate. Go through the gate and then keep
along the track, which descends
through trees to a T-junction.

Turn left and go through a metal
kissing-gate, beside a lodge, on to the
road. Turn right downhill to return to
Port Askaig. ●

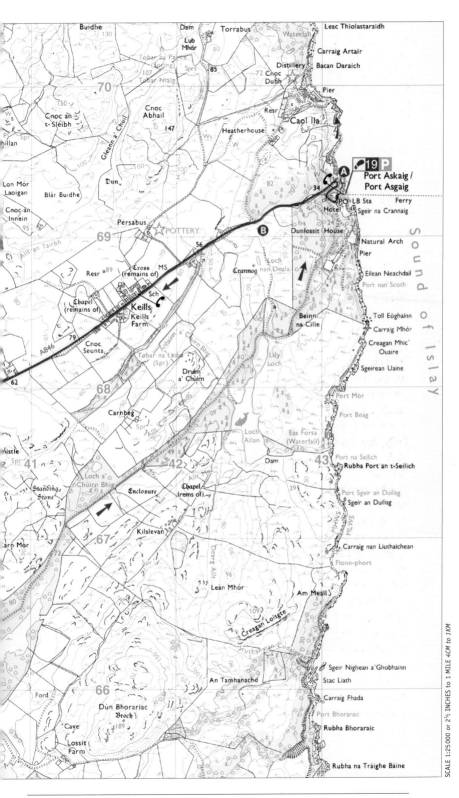

SCALE 1:25,000 or 2½ INCHES to 1 MILE 4CM to 1KM

Isle of Ulva

Start	Ulva, Boathouse Visitor Centre and Tearoom
Distance	7½ miles (12.1km) Shorter version 4½ miles (7.2km)
Approximate time	4 hours (2½ hours for shorter walk)
Parking	Ulva ferry terminal on Mull, just off B8073
Refreshments	Tearoom at Boathouse Visitor Centre
Ordnance Survey maps	Landranger 47 (Tobermory & North Mull), Explorers 374 (Isle of Mull North & Tobermory) and 375 (Isle of Mull East)

Ulva is a private island, reached by a ferry crossing of a few minutes from Mull. There are no tarmac roads and no cars, but a number of well-waymarked paths and tracks, all starting from the Boathouse Visitor Centre and Tearoom by the pier, guide visitors around a number of circular routes. This walk combines several of these and explores the eastern part of the island. From many points there are outstanding views both of Ulva's coastline and looking across Loch na Keal to the mountains of Mull, dominated by Ben More. Some of the paths are rocky and care is required; some are overgrown and in places almost engulfed by bracken, but they are generally obvious.

Between mid-October and mid-April the ferry runs by arrangement only. During the rest of the year there is a regular service on demand from Monday to Friday, and on Sunday during June, July and August. When the weather is bad, it is always best to check if it is running by phoning 01688 500226/500264.

Around the middle of the 19th century there were over 600 inhabitants on the isle of Ulva, mainly engaged in crofting, fishing and the kelp industry. Kelp is created from burning seaweed and was used at the time in the manufacture of glass and soap. A combination of potato blight and the collapse of the kelp markets led to the Clearances, when most of the crofters were evicted from their homes, and now

the population of the island is only around 25.

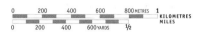 Start in front of the Boathouse Tearoom and, facing the sea, turn left along a track which curves to the left. At a footpath sign, turn left **Ⓐ**, in 'Farm Circuit Clockwise' direction, along a track, go through a gate and continue, initially through trees and later across a meadow. On the far side of the meadow, follow the track to the left, by woodland on the right, and then curve right to reach another footpath sign.

Turn left, in 'Wood/Shore' direction, on to a track, and where it bends right, keep ahead along a path which descends to a gate. Go through and follow a winding uphill path through woodland, later continuing between trees and bracken and bending right on the edge of the trees. Turn sharp left through a metal gate, almost doubling

back, and continue along a coast path, narrow and overgrown at times but well-waymarked with regular white posts and white blobs on rocks. The path winds up and down the low cliffs through a mixture of grass, bracken and woodland, following the curve of the coast to the right. At one point it descends to climb a ladder-stile, and look out for a footpath sign where you bear left, in the 'Basalt Columns, Livingstone Croft, Wood/Shore Walk' direction. Much of this part of the walk is along raised platforms above the shore with a line of low cliffs to the right. The views stretching ahead along the wild and rocky south coast of Ulva are superb, and there are a number of tiny islands.

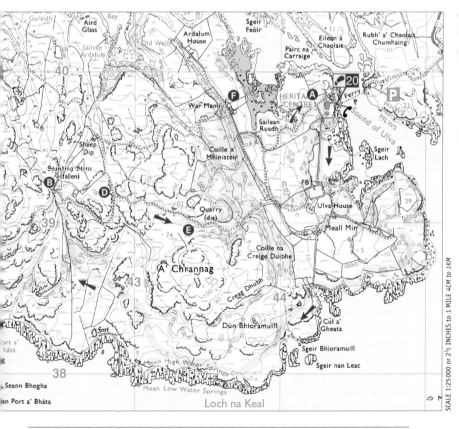

Ulva's magnificent coastline

Eventually the path bears right, away from the coast, and climbs to a gap in the line of low cliffs. Continue through the gap, descend into a valley and follow the white-waymarked route around several twists and turns, heading up to a ruined cottage. This is Livingstone's Croft, home of Dr David Livingstone's parents and grandparents. Turn right, continue steadily uphill between rocks, bracken and woodland to the head of the valley, and at the top descend to a track **B**.

*At this point the shorter walk turns right here and continues from **B** below.*

For the full walk, turn left along the winding track which keeps parallel to the coast and descends to the bay at Cragaig **C** where there is a ruined mill building. The views across the islet-studded bay are magnificent.

Retrace your steps to where you joined the track at **B**, here rejoining the route of the shorter walk. Continue along the track – a standing stone can be seen below on the left – heading downhill and winding round to a footpath post **D**. Turn right, in the 'Ferry' direction, and ahead is a superb view of the mountains on Mull. Just before reaching the edge of woodland, turn left **E**, at a footpath sign marked 'Wood/Shore Walk', along a narrow path that heads up through bracken. The path continues through a mixture of bracken and trees, turns right to keep beside a wire fence on the left and descends to a footpath post at a junction of paths. On the descent, the fine views ahead are of the north coast of Ulva, with Mull beyond across the waters of Loch Tuath.

At the path junction keep ahead, going uphill in the 'Wood/Shore Walk, Church, Ferry' direction, and the path later curves right and zigzags down through woodland to a metal gate. Go through and keep ahead to a track by the church, designed by Thomas Telford and built 1827-8. Turn right **F** along the attractive, tree-lined track, and at the next footpath post turn left, in the 'Ferry' direction, to follow the track back to the starting point. ●

Ardmore and Glengorm

Start	Forestry Commission's Ardmore car park – from Tobermory take the Dervaig road, turn off along side road to Glengorm and turn right on to track on edge of forest
Distance	8 miles (12.9km)
Approximate time	4 hours
Parking	Ardmore car park
Refreshments	None
Ordnance Survey maps	Landranger 47 (Tobermory & North Mull), Explorer 374 (Isle of Mull North & Tobermory)

Most of this fairly lengthy but easy route is along clear tracks and paths through conifer woodland, with forays into more open country that provide some grand views across the water to the remote peninsula of Ardnamurchan and the isle of Coll. One particularly outstanding viewpoint is Ardmore Bay, and another is a strategically placed bench beside the forest track between Ardmore Bay and Glengorm.

🖊 Start by walking along the wide track by the right edge of the forest, part of the Ardmore – Glengorm Mountain

Ardnamurchan from Ardmore Point

Bike Route, passing through several metal gates and following red waymarks. Descend to enter the forest via a metal gate, and at a fork take the right-hand track **Ⓐ**, here leaving the cycle route.

Continue along the red-waymarked route – ignoring all side turns – and the track later narrows to a grassy path. Turn right in front of a ruined cottage to ford a burn, then turn left and keep beside the burn. The abandoned buildings around here are the remains of the former village of Ardmore. After descending through dark, densely packed conifers, you suddenly emerge on to the coast at Ardmore Bay 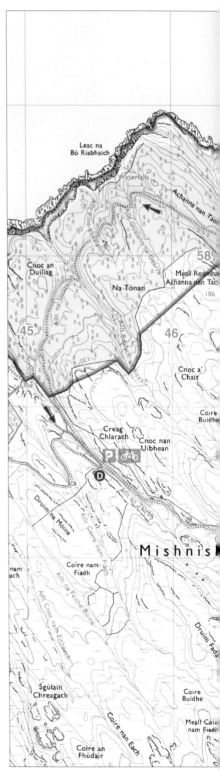. To the right is Ardmore Point, and there is a superb view across Ardmore Bay to the mountainous Ardnamurchan Peninsula.

The path curves left between bracken to keep beside the shore, and you follow a series of red-waymarked posts across rough ground – an area of felled forest – ascending a low cliff, fording a burn and climbing up another low cliff. At the end of the bay, the path turns left, heads uphill and re-enters the forest. On meeting a broad track, turn right **Ⓒ**, rejoining the cycle route, and follow this winding and undulating track through the conifers. At one point there is a lovely view across the sea to the isle of Coll, and a bench enables you to appreciate it in comfort.

Look out for a fork where the main track continues to the left – follow it and eventually you reach a gate on the edge of the forest. Go through, and as you continue across open country the 19th-century Glengorm Castle can be seen over to the right. Climb a stile, keep ahead and the track emerges on to a narrow road by Glengorm car park **Ⓓ**. Continue along the road for just over two miles (3.2km), initially uphill, later descending and re-entering the forest. At a red-waymarked post where the road bends right, turn left along a track to the start. ●

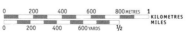

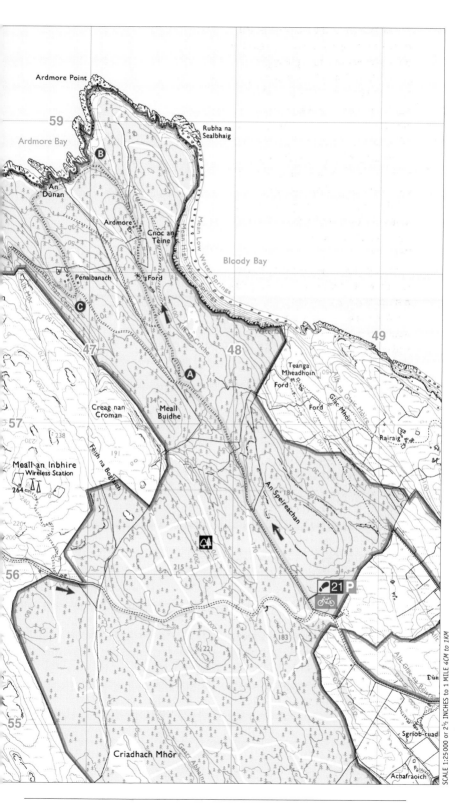

Ardmore Point

59

Ardmore Bay

Rubha na
Sealbhaig

An
Dùnan

B

Ardmore

Cnoc an
Tèine

Bloody Bay

Pennalbanach

Ford

C

49

Waterfall

47

48

Teanga
Mheadhoin

Ford

Ford

Creag nan
Croman

Meall
Buidhe

Rairaig

57

238

191

Meall an Inbhire
Wireless Station

264

An Speireachan

184

56

170

21 P

183

55

Dùn

Sgriob-ruad

Criadhach Mhôr

Achafraoich

SCALE 1:25000 or 2½ INCHES to 1 MILE 4CM to 1KM

Carradale

Start	Carradale, Forestry Commission's Port na Storm car park on western edge of village
Distance	7½ miles (12.1km) Shorter version 6½ miles (10.5km)
Approximate time	4 hours (3½ hours for shorter walk)
Parking	Port na Storm car park at Carradale
Refreshments	None en route but a hotel in nearby Carradale
Ordnance Survey maps	Landranger 69 (Isle of Arran), Explorer 356 (Kintyre South)

This circuit, to the north of the village of Carradale, is mostly through forest but also includes a short stretch of coastline and a climb across moorland slopes to the 756ft (230m) summit of Cnoc nan Gabhar (Deer Hill), a magnificent viewpoint. Throughout the walk there are many spectacular views, particularly over Kilbrannan Sound to the mountains of Arran, across Carradale Bay, and down the gentle, wooded Carradale Glen. The shorter walk returns directly to the start and omits the climb to Cnoc nan Gabhar.

Take the blue- and red-waymarked track – Shore Walk – that leads off from the car park through conifers, turn right at a T-junction and keep along the right edge of the forest. For most of the route you follow blue waymarks.

The track later re-enters conifer woodland – look out for where a blue waymark directs you to bear right **A** along a path, initially by a fence on the right, which winds through the trees, crosses several footbridges and heads steeply downhill to the shore.

Turn left and keep by the shore – sometimes along the right inside edge of the trees and sometimes across the stony beach. This is a lovely, wild and unspoilt stretch of coast with grand views across the water to the mountains of Arran. Eventually a blue waymark directs

you to the left and you head uphill away from the beach into the forest again. Go up steps and follow the winding path between rock faces and through trees, turning right to emerge on to a track. Continue along it and from this elevated position there are good views across Kilbrannon Sound to Arran. As the track gently descends and curves left, fine views open up ahead of Carradale Glen. At a fork take the left-hand, lower track which narrows to a path and continues down to the road at Grianon car park and picnic site **B**.

At the car park turn sharp left, almost doubling back, along a broad track. Shortly after climbing a stile, the track bends right and contours along the

0	200	400	600	800 METRES	**1**
					KILOMETRES
					MILES
0	200	400	600 YARDS	½	

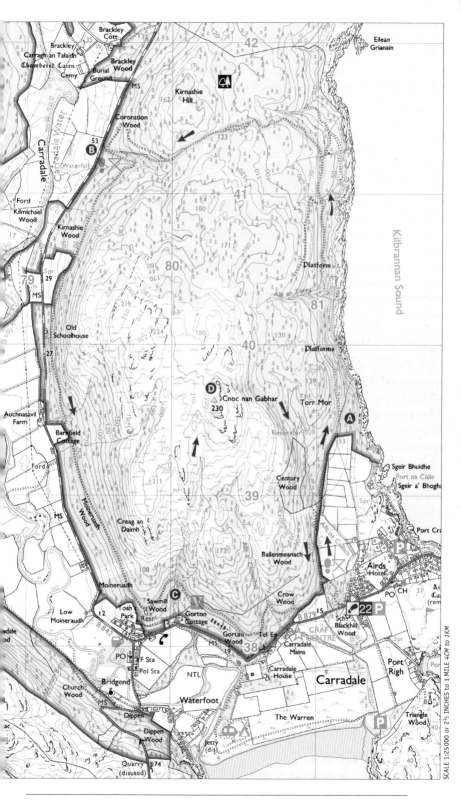

wooded hillside. Over to the right are attractive views of the green and well-wooded Carradale Glen. After nearly two miles (3.2km), the track bends left, and where the track then curves right  **C** , the full and shorter versions of the walk divide.

For the short walk simply continue along the track, turning right where you rejoin the outward route to return along the track to the start.

If you are doing the full walk, turn left at a Deer Hill Walk post – now following red waymarks – on to a path that heads steeply uphill through the trees, later winding across rocky, heathery, bracken-covered moorland. At a red-waymarked post, a brief detour to the left brings you to the triangulation pillar at the top of Cnoc nan Gabhar **D**, which is a superb panoramic viewpoint over coast, forest and glen.

Return to the main path, turn left and follow it as it winds downhill to a gate. Go through the gate, keep ahead to go through another one and descend to a track. Turn right, here rejoining the outward route, and retrace your steps back to the start.

Rugged coastline near Carradale

Bowmore and Loch Indaal

Start	Bowmore
Distance	8½ miles (13.7km)
Approximate time	4 hours
Parking	Bowmore
Refreshments	Pubs and café at Bowmore
Ordnance Survey maps	Landranger 60 (Islay), Explorers 352 (Islay South) and 353 (Islay North)

Much of the walk is along or close to the shores of Loch Indaal on the west coast of Islay, and there is a succession of grand views across the loch to the houses of Bruichladdich and Port Charlotte, backed by a typically bare and austere Hebridean landscape. There is also some fine cliff scenery, and later come impressive views, both down the long sandy stretch of Big Strand and across the flat expanses of the island to the striking and unmistakeable profile of the Paps of Jura.

The small town of Bowmore, capital of Islay, is pleasantly situated on Loch Indaal and dominated by its famous distillery and the Round Church. The latter stands at the top of the main street which leads down to the harbour. Built in 1767, its circular shape was to ensure that the devil could not find any corners in which to hide.

🥾 Start at the Square at the bottom end of Main Street and walk up the street to the church. Pass to the right of the church, in the Port Ellen direction, and take the first turning on the right **Ⓐ** to continue along a lane.

At a T-junction turn left along a lane, go through a series of metal gates and, where the lane turns left to enter a landfill site,

keep ahead along a track. Follow the track as it heads towards the shores of Loch Indaal, going through two more gates. Just before reaching a metal gate at the entrance to the ruined Gartbreck

Loch Indaal

Farm, turn left across the grass, go through a metal gate and turn left **B** to continue along a track by the shores of the loch.

The track later peters out, and you keep across the springy turf to a metal gate. Go through the gate, keep ahead and after passing to the right of a ruined building, you continue along a particularly impressive stretch of rocky coastline, later picking up a definite track again.

The track winds between rocks and then bears left away from the coast and heads up over rough heathland. On the horizon the outlines of the mountains on the isle of Jura can be seen. On reaching the reedy Lochan na Nigheadaireachd, the track turns left alongside it and follows the lochan's edge to the right. Go through a gate, keep ahead to a T-junction and turn left along a track **C**.

Go through a metal gate – the track curves right, passing farm buildings, then turns left through a metal gate and continues above the sea. To the right is the glorious – and usually deserted – long sandy beach of Big Strand. Pass through a wall gap, at a fork take the left-hand track and follow it – going through several more metal gates – to a road **D**. Turn left along the road for ³⁄₄ mile (1.2km) and about 50 yds (46m) after passing a track on the right, turn left **E** along a straight, hedge- and tree-lined track which heads back towards Loch Indaal.

At a T-junction turn right along a lane, here rejoining the outward route, and retrace your steps back to the start. On this final leg of the walk there is a particularly striking view of the Round Church at Bowmore, with the Paps of Jura in the background.

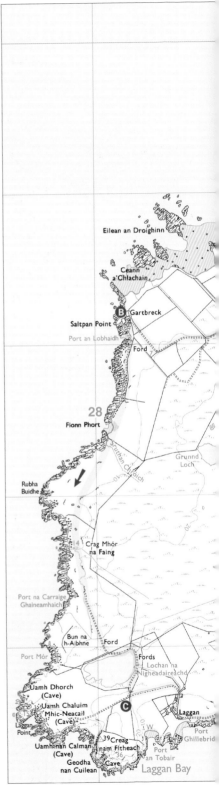

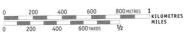

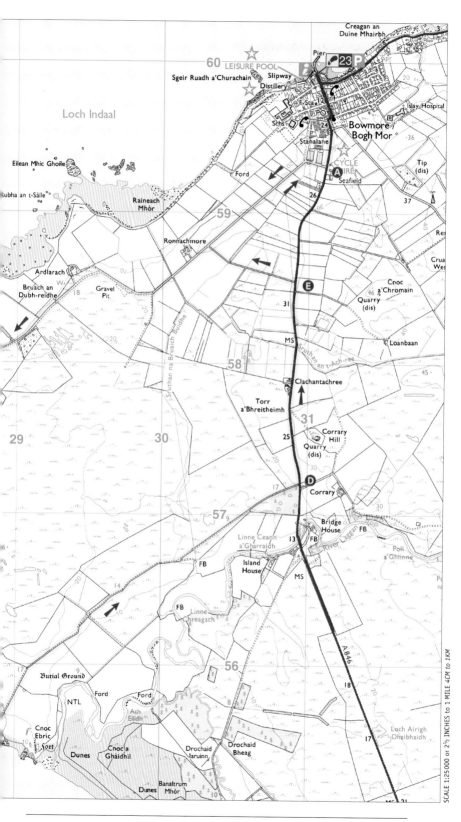

Loch Indaal

Eilean Mhic Ghoile

Rubha an t-Sàile

Raineach Mhór

Ardlarach

Bruach an Dubh-reidhe

Gravel Pit

Ronnachmore

Ford

Creagan an Duine Mhairbh

Pier

23 P

60 LEISURE POOL

Sgeir Ruadh a'Churachain

Slipway

Distillery

F. Sta.

PO

Schs

Stanalane

Islay Hospital

Bowmore / Bogh Mor

CYCLE HIRE

A

Seafield

59

26

Cnoc a'Chromain

Quarry (dis)

Tip (dis)

Res

Crua West

E

58

31

MS

Sruthan an t-Ach-ree

Loanbaan

Sruthan na Bruaich Buidhe

Clachantachree

Torr a'Bhreitheimh

31

Corrary Hill

Quarry (dis)

29

30

25

D

Corrary

57

Bridge House

FB

Linne Ceann a'Gharraidh

Island House

River Laggan

Poll a'Ghinne

MS

FB

Linne Chreagach

FB

56

Burial Ground

NTL

Ford

Ford

Ath Eilidh

A 846

Cnoc Ebric Sort

Dunes

Cnoc a Ghàidhil

Drochaid Iaruinn

Drochaid Bheag

Loch Airigh Dheibhaidh

Dunes

Banaltrum Mhòr

SCALE 1:25000 or 2½ INCHES to 1 MILE 4CM to 1KM

Isle of Iona

Start	Iona, by ferry terminal
Distance	8½ miles (13.7km), or two separate walks of 3½ miles (5.6km) and 5 miles (8km)
Approximate time	4½ hours (2 hours and 2½ hours for the two shorter walks)
Parking	By the ferry terminal at Fionnphort
Refreshments	Hotels and cafés on Iona
Ordnance Survey maps	Landranger 48 (Iona & West Mull), Explorer 373 (Iona, Staffa & Ross of Mull)

This walk can obviously be divided into two separate walks, and there are short detours that can be omitted, but the full walk is eminently worthwhile and enjoyable as it explores a large proportion of Iona and includes all four of the island's coasts. The walking is easy as Iona is fairly flat, and you are advised to take your time in order to appreciate fully not only the excellent scenery, beautiful beaches and magnificent views, but also the sense of isolation, rich historical significance and fascinating collection of religious buildings of this unique and highly atmospheric holy isle.

'That man is little to be envied... whose piety would not grow warmer amongst the ruins of Iona'. Few would disagree with those words, spoken by Doctor Johnson while on a visit here in the 18th century. Since 563, when St Columba landed on Iona from Ireland on his evangelising mission to Scotland, this small island lying off the south-west tip of Mull has been a major religious centre. A monastery grew up, probably on the site of Columba's first church, and in the early 16th century this became the cathedral of the bishops of the Isles. After the Reformation the church and monastic buildings were neglected and gradually fell into ruin, but from 1938 onwards, under the inspired leadership of George MacLeod, a Glasgow minister, the abbey was

restored and rebuilt as a centre of ecumenical worship and study. The abbey church and former cathedral, which lay in ruins for over four centuries, mainly dates from the 13th and 15th centuries. A small but dignified pink granite building, it is the chief landmark on the island.

Near the abbey/cathedral is a remarkable collection of other ecclesiastical monuments. The 11th-century St Oran's Chapel has a superb Norman doorway and stands amidst an ancient burial ground that is alleged to contain the now vanished graves of over 60 kings – Scottish, Irish and Norse. On the edge of the village are the impressive ruins of a Benedictine nunnery, surrounded by an attractive garden. Between the chapel and nunnery stands Maclean's Cross, probably erected in the 15th century, and next to it is Thomas Telford's plain, early 19th-century parish church.

From the ferry terminal keep ahead through the small village of Baile Mór – the only settlement on the island – and take the first turning on the right. Walk along a tarmac track in front of a row of cottages, continue along a rough track, go through a kissing-gate and keep by a wall on the left. At a wall corner, turn left towards the abbey, go up steps and walk along the south side of the church. Turn right across the west front, bear left and go through a gate in the right-hand corner of the abbey grounds in front of the Iona Community Coffee House.

Turn right **A** along a narrow road and just after passing between houses, turn left through a metal gate **B** in order to make a detour to the summit of Dùn I, the only hill on the island and a fine viewpoint. Bear left at the base of the hill, then bear right and head uphill, making your way to the cairn and triangulation pillar at the top. Despite a height of only 333ft (101m), the extensive view takes in the whole of Iona, some of the nearby islands (including Staffa) and the west coast of Mull, with Ben More on the skyline. Retrace your steps downhill to the road **B**, turn left and continue along it.

Where the road bends left to a farm, keep ahead through a gate, at a National Trust for Scotland sign marked 'Footpath to North Shore', and walk along a track. Continue across grass to the north coast of the island and turn left through the dunes to continue along the beautiful, sandy beach of Tràigh an t-Suidhe. Turn left through a metal gate **C** and head back up across the grassy headland to rejoin the track.

Retrace your steps along the track and the road, then continue along the road, passing the abbey, St Oran's Chapel, parish church, Maclean's Cross and nunnery, to reach a T-junction by the corner of the nunnery wall **D**.

If only doing the northern (3½ mile/5.6km) circuit, turn left here to return to the starting point. Those doing just the southern (5 mile/8km) circuit, keep ahead along the road from the ferry terminal to join the full walk at this point.

At the T-junction turn right. Where the road ends, turn left through a metal gate and walk along a track which heads gently uphill and curves right. Turn left by a group of farm buildings, go through a metal gate and continue along a straight track to a crossroads **E**. Turn right along a narrow road towards the west coast and, where the

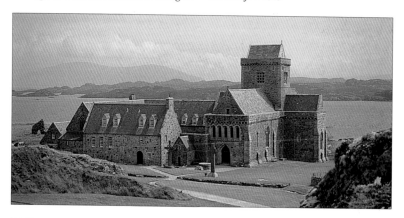

The Abbey on Iona

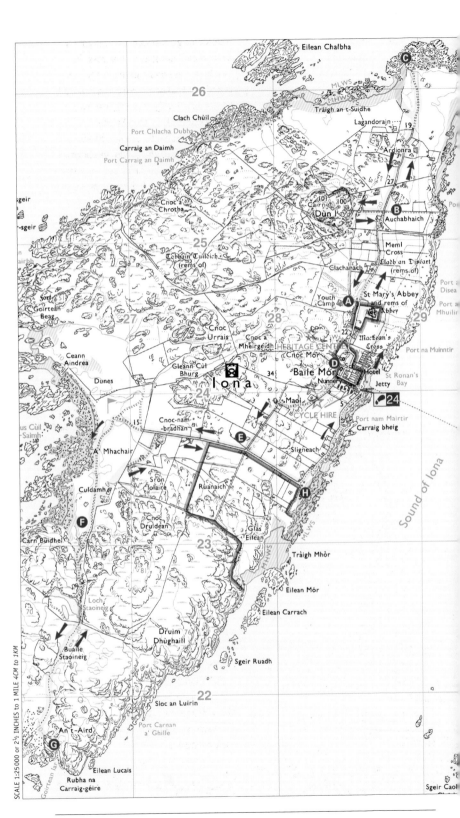

Eilean Chalbha

26

C

Tràig an t-Suidhe

MLWS
MHWS

Clach Chùil
Port Chlacha Dubha

Lagandorain

19

Carraig an Daimh

Ardionra

Port Carraig an Daimh

27

25

101
Càirn
100
Dùn I

B

Auchabhaich

-sgeir

airbh

Tobhain Tuildich
(rems of)

Clachanach

Meml
Cross

Port a
Disea

sgeir

70

Cladh an Diseart
(rems of)

Sort
Goirtean
Beag

27

Cnoc
Urrais

28

Youth
Camp

A

St Mary's Abbey
and rems of
Abbey

Port a
Mhuiltr

29

Ceann
Aindrea

Cnoc a'
Chrotha

Cnoc a'
Mheirgeidh

HERITAGE CENTRE

22

MacLean's
Cross

Port na Muinntir

Dunes

Gleann Cùl
Bhurg

Iona

Cnoc Mór

D

Baile Mór

Hotel

St Ronan's
Bay

us Cùil
Saimh

34

Nunnery

Jetty

15

A'Mhachair

Cnoc-nam-
bradhan

Maol

CYCLE HIRE

5

24

Port nam Mairtir

Carraig bheig

E

Sligneach

24

Culdamh

Sròn
Tiolaire

Ruanaich

H

Cnoc
Druidean

Glas
Eilean

Carn Buidhe

F

23

Tràigh Mhòr

Loch
Staoineig

Eilean Mór

Eilean Carrach

Druim
Dhùghaill

76

Sgeir Ruadh

Buaile
Staoineig

22

Sloc an Luirin

Port Carnan
a' Ghille

An t-Aird

G

Eilean Lucais

Rubha na
Carraig-gèire

Sgeir Caol

SCALE 1:25000 or 2½ INCHES to 1 MILE 4CM to 1KM

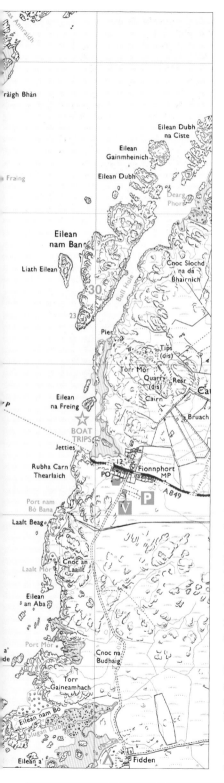

road ends, go through a metal gate and keep ahead along a track across the machair – the name given to the lush grassland that grows on the sandy soil here – to a lovely, curving, sandy bay called Camus Cuil an t-Saimh.

Turn left to walk along the low headland above the beach and bear left across the machair to join a stony track **F**. Turn right and follow the track over a ridge to reach a lochan (Loch Staoineig) at the top.

Keep to the left of the lochan, by a wire fence on the right, continue across heathery moorland – there are boardwalks in places – and the path descends, quite steeply at one point, and heads across flat grassland to Port na Curaich on the south coast of the island **G**. Also known as St Columba's Bay, this is where the saint is alleged to have made his landing in 563.

Retrace your steps back over the ridge and past the lochan. From the top of the ridge there is a superb view along the west coast. Instead of returning to the beach at **F**, continue along the track and, where the track peters out at the bottom, keep straight ahead across the machair, by a wire fence on the right. After the wire fence turns right, continue ahead across part of a golf course, following a series of short posts and passing to the left of a house. When you see a metal gate, turn right to go through it and head towards a cottage. Pass to the right of the cottage, go through a metal gate on to a road, here rejoining the previous route, and continue as far as **E**.

For an alternative route back, do not turn left along the track here but keep ahead along the road, which bends left on reaching the coast **H** and continues back to the start. ⬤

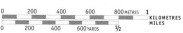

Crinan Canal and Knapdale Forest

Crinan Canal and Knapdale Forest

Start	Crinan. Shorter walk starts at the Forestry Commission car park and picnic site at Dunardry, point **E**
Distance	9 miles (14.5km) Shorter version 4½ miles (7.2km)
Approximate time	4 hours (2 hours for shorter walk)
Parking	Crinan, by canal basin
Refreshments	Hotel and coffee shop at Crinan
Ordnance Survey maps	Landranger 55 (Lochgilphead & Loch Awe), Explorer 358 (Lochgilphead & Knapdale North)

The first and last parts of the walk are along the towpath of the beautiful Crinan Canal; the middle section is a climb through the mixed woodlands of Knapdale Forest at the north end of the Kintyre Peninsula. A brief detour at the top brings you to a superb viewpoint overlooking coast, forests, the marshland of Mòine Mhór and the rock of Dunadd. The shorter version omits the section along the canal to and from the canal basin at Crinan.

The Crinan Canal is just nine miles (14.5km) long and cuts across the narrow isthmus at the top of the Kintyre Peninsula. It was built at the height of the canal boom in 1793 in order to avoid the long journey around the Mull of Kintyre and bring the produce of the Western Isles and the west coast of Scotland closer to the markets of Glasgow and the Clyde. Financial and constructional problems delayed its completion until 1809 and the canal never fully achieved the high commercial hopes of its founders. Today the Crinan Canal is mainly used by leisure craft, and the towpath provides superb walking. The canal basin at Crinan at the western end, where the walk starts, is a delightful spot, used by yachts and fishing boats.

Begin by walking down beside the canal basin and turn right over lock 15 on to the towpath. Keep along the towpath as far as the second swing bridge – at Bellanoch – a distance of about two miles (3.2km). This is a most attractive part of the walk – there are views to the left across Loch Crinan and the broad sands of the estuary of the River Add, and ½ mile (800m) before Bellanoch, the canal widens out into another basin.

Turn right over the bridge, **A**, turn left along the road and after ¼ mile (400m) – where the road curves left – turn right on to a track **B**. Head uphill and where the track turns sharply right go straight ahead through a metal gate and onto a forest road. Continue along this winding road ignoring the grass track branching off to the right. At the next junction leave the forest track and turn right onto a narrow path which enters woodland, then emerges onto open ground before ending at a T-junction beside some houses. Turn left onto the forest track here and continue along it ignoring all turn offs, particularly one on the left which passes a quarry. When the track turns sharply right near an old slate quarry which may only be visible in winter, turn left at the yellow waymarker for a brief detour to a viewpoint. The path ascends the steep hillside, via steps and with railings and boardwalks in places,

The canal basin, Crinan

to reach a triangulation pillar at the top ⊙. Despite its modest height, 705ft (214m), the views from here are impressive and extensive: to the west along the Crinan Canal to an island-studded sea dominated by the Paps of Jura, and to the north looking across Mòine Mhór (Great Moss) and the winding River Add. The prominent rock ahead is Dunadd, the site of an Iron Age

fort and the capital of the kingdom of Dalriada, which was founded by the Scots after they landed in Argyll from Ireland in the 6th century. It was the later merging of the Picts and Scots that created the kingdom of Scotland.

As you retrace your steps downhill,

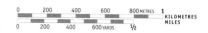

Crinan Canal

more fine views open up of the forests stretching southwards down the Kintyre Peninsula. On regaining the track, turn left – it soon becomes a tarmac track – and descend to a T-junction in front of waterfalls. Turn left, continue downhill beside Dunardry Burn and look out for a yellow footprint symbol on a post where you turn left on to a path. Head up steps and follow the clear and well-waymarked path through the tall, dark and tightly packed conifers, descending via boardwalks and steps at times, and still with the cascading burn below. Later continue along a grassy ledge and descend to a track **D**. Turn sharp right and follow it downhill to the Forestry Commission car park at Dunardry **E**.

*The shorter walk starts here and initially follows route directions to Bellanoch Bridge **A**.*

Descend steps to the road, turn left and after 200 yds (183m), turn sharp right on to a path, initially doubling back, then turning left over a footbridge and climbing steps to cross the Crinan Canal by lock 9.

Turn left on to the towpath **F** and follow it alongside the Dunardry flight of locks, with the flat expanses of Mòine Mhór over to the right. Mòine Mhór, or the Great Moss, is a National Nature Reserve and one of the largest intact examples of peatland left in Britain. Continue past the Dunardry swing bridge and on to Bellanoch Bridge **A**.

*Those doing the shorter walk turn left over the bridge and follow route directions from **A** to **E**.*

Here the full walk rejoins the outward route and continues along the towpath back to Crinan. Towards the end come superb views across Loch Crinan to the outlines of the Paps of Jura.

Beinn Bheula

Start	Glenbranter, Forestry Commission's Lauder car park
Distance	9½ miles (15.3km)
Approximate time	6 hours
Parking	Lauder car park, Glenbranter
Refreshments	None
Ordnance Survey maps	Landranger 56 (Loch Lomond & Inveraray), Explorer 363 (Cowal East)

The first and last parts of the walk are along roads and clear, well-surfaced forest tracks; the middle section of the walk is across rough, open, pathless moorland and hillside. This middle part is basically a circle that follows a series of peaks and cols, reaching its greatest height at the summit of Beinn Bheula (2556 ft/779m). From here and from many other points on the route, the extensive views over the Argyll Forest Park, Loch Goil, Loch Eck, Glenbranter and the hills of Cowal are magnificent and well worth the effort. However, this is a strenuous walk that requires good visibility and on no account should it be attempted in bad weather, especially misty conditions, unless you are experienced and equipped for such conditions and able to navigate by using a compass.

From the car park walk back along the main track which bends right to a lane. Turn left, cross a bridge over the River Cur and, at a T-junction, turn right along the main road. Just after passing a sign to the Lauder Monument, turn left on to a forest track **Ⓐ**, by a metal marker post indicating 15 miles to Dunoon Pier.

The Lauders were local landowners and it was from the well-known Scottish entertainer, Sir Harry Lauder, that the Forestry Commission first obtained a lease to begin the planting of their forests in Cowal in the 1920s.

The track bends right, bends left to pass through a metal gate, then bends right again and heads steadily uphill.

Ignore the first track on the left, turn sharply left along the second track, continue uphill and take the first turning on the right, another sharp turn. Then go round an equally sharp left-hand bend **Ⓑ** and continue up to where the track ends on the edge of the forest. Turn right to go through a gate **Ⓒ** and ahead are the steep slopes of Carnach Mór.

The next part of the walk involves some rough and tiring hillwalking, with several burns to ford, damp conditions underfoot, a number of ascents and descents and no visible paths.

Descend steeply to ford a burn – this could be difficult after wet weather – and head up the grassy slopes to the

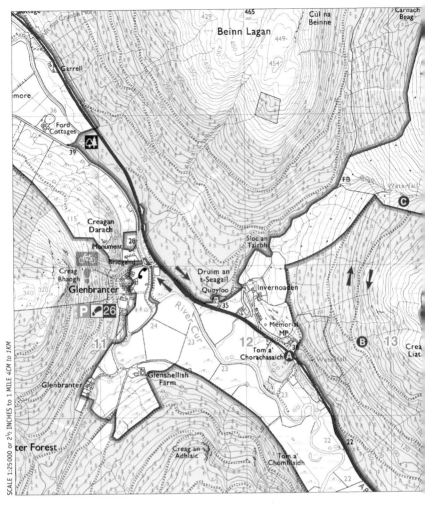

SCALE 1:25000 or 2½ INCHES to 1 MILE 4CM to 1KM

0 200 400 600 800 METRES 1
                                            KILOMETRES
                                            MILES
0 200 400 600 YARDS ½

rocks on Carnach Mór. Turn right to follow a broad ridge, bear right to descend to a gap in the ridge and then head steeply uphill again to the triangulation pillar on the summit of Beinn Bheula **D**. On a clear day the all-round views are superb and take in Loch Goil, much of the Argyll Forest Park, Loch Eck, Glenbranter and the hills of Cowal. Nearer at hand the small but beautiful Curra Lochain lies below.

Continue a little farther along the ridge and then turn right to descend across more rough ground into the col between Beinn Bheula and the distinctive, conical peak of Beinn Dubhain, in sight for much of the way. Keep ahead to climb to the summit of Beinn Dubhain (2130ft/649m) **E**, which offers more magnificent views, especially looking down the length of Loch Eck towards the Firth of Clyde.

On the descent bear right, making for the edge of the conifers. On reaching the forest fence, turn right and keep alongside it across rough, boggy and uneven ground, following it around a left bend to the gate where you left the forest **C**. Go through, here picking up the outward route, and retrace your steps downhill to the start, enjoying more grand views of Glenbranter and Loch Eck.

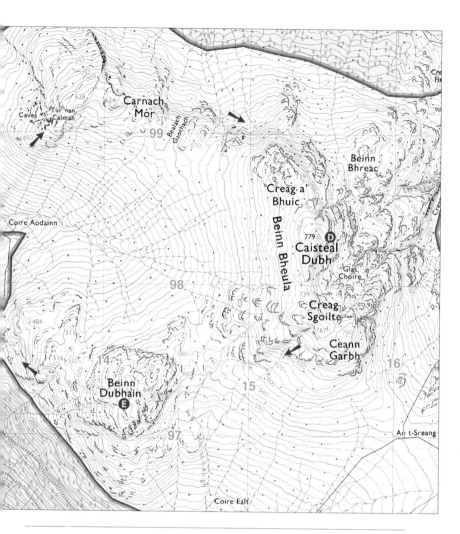

Loch Eck from Beinn Bheula

The Ben Cruachan Horseshoe

Start	Cruachan power station
Distance	8 miles (12.9km)
Approximate time	8 hours
Parking	Lay-bys on main road near power station
Refreshments	None
Ordnance Survey maps	Landranger 50 (Glen Orchy & Loch Etive), Explorers 377 (Loch Etive & Glen Orchy) and 360 (Loch Awe & Inveraray)

Make no mistake: this route provides a major challenge even for the experienced walker. *The total height climbed in walking the seven summits is well over 5000ft (1524m) and the rocky parts of the traverse require some scrambling. Perhaps the worst of it is that the climbing is not finished even when Ben Cruachan has been captured: the route down takes in the lesser summit of Meall Cuanail, a formidable obstacle after what has come before. Man has adapted the landscape here to his own needs and the great reservoir is testament to this. The most remarkable part of this work, however, is screened from view below the waters of Loch Awe and beneath the mountain itself – this is sometimes called the Hollow Mountain because of the chamber excavated inside it to house the generators. At some point try to make time to visit the Cruachan power station: it will be all the more impressive if you have intimate knowledge of the mountain which gives it both its name and the water to power its turbines.* To check on access to this route during the stalking season telephone 01838 200217.

The obvious place to park would seem to be the visitor centre car park at the power station, but since it closes at 4.45pm it is of little use to climbers undertaking this demanding route. There is off-road parking reasonably close to the start.

🖊 The route begins at a track which leaves the main road opposite the staff car park of the power station, about 100 yards (90m) east of the entrance to the public car park. The track gives access to a railway crossing through a kissing-gate. Then a path climbs steeply up the west bank of a burn, oaks and birches screening the view at first. However, after a few minutes it will be necessary to pause for breath, and by this time enough height will have been gained to allow views over Loch Awe.

The reservoir from Ben Cruachan

This is a steep and unrelenting ascent accompanied by the soothing sound of the burn, which is never very far away.

The best views back are from the tree-line where the path levels out. If the burn is not in spate it is possible to cut a corner here **Ⓐ** by heading for the pylon below the hydro road on the right, climbing up a grassy bank from the stream to reach the road and thus avoiding a dog-leg. Turn left on to the road and then fork right to reach the eastern side of Cruachan Reservoir. Before the tunnel entrance **Ⓑ** (where the track ends) climb a little way up the slopes of the hill and then follow the contours northwards.

Keep fairly low on the flank of the hill to ford two streams, the second, major, one coming down from Lairig Torran, the access point for the ridge. Make the most of the cold sparkling water here **Ⓒ**: there are few streams once the ridge is gained.

The climbing is steady from here, eastwards, following the stream at first up a grassy slope. Beyond the source of the burn is the Lairig Torran, a pass used by drovers before the building of the reservoir. In those days the ground now covered by water was valuable summer pasture.

Turn northwards at the col **Ⓓ** and then continue to climb, making for a cairn on the skyline which sports a metal post from its centre. This is one of several false summits, but soon afterwards you will be on the ridge enjoying a fabulous view which extends over most of the Southern Highlands. Beinn Bhuidhe is the dominant summit to the south-east.

Although the ridge looks daunting, walking along it is exhilarating. For about 200 yds (182m) the path which heads northwards is level, but then it

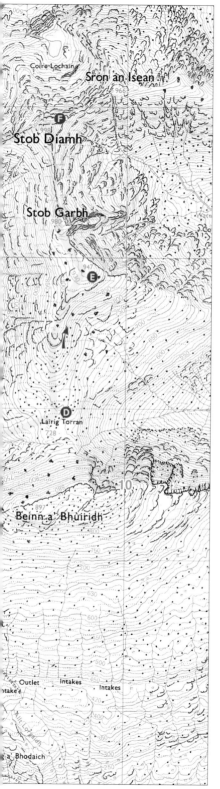

loses itself amongst scattered rock before the climb to the first notable summit . After this there are precipitous slopes to the right; snow can remain piled against these crags until midsummer. Each succeeding summit offers a better view. After a cairn the path drops down steeply amongst boulders – in places it is becoming eroded. There is a handsome cairn on top of the next ridge – above Coire Lochain – where the path swings through 90° to head west . Loch Etive can be seen now, and, on a clear day, Ben Nevis. This height can suffer badly from midges, even in May with snow still on the ground.

From here the route descends to an exciting feature – a narrow ridge hardly wider than Striding Edge in the Lake District. After the last level section of this skywalk the path disintegrates and the walker is left with a scramble to surmount the massive scattered boulders of Drochaid Ghlas. It is important to keep to the path (such as it is) even though it comes close to the edge at times. Now the summit of Cruachan is revealed in all its glory. After a short easy stretch along a ridge only a few metres wide the final assault on the summit commences. Smooth boulders left tilted at steep angles present a challenging obstacle, and some may feel the best way to tackle them is in an undignified seated position. The top of Ben Cruachan is only a short scramble away from this last hazard to ankles and nerves.

The view is outstanding: on a clear day the distinctive domed shape of Ben Nevis is easily identifiable to the north, as is the conical form of Ben Starav to the north-east, though some closer heights are less easy to recognise. All of

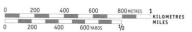

Loch Etive and most of Loch Awe can also be seen.

However, there is one summit which is almost too easy to identify and which has been lurking menacingly at the back of the mind ever since the ridge was reached. To get off Ben Cruachan one last peak has to be claimed – Meall Cuanail – and after this time and distance its steep slope looks formidable. It may be for this reason that people do not linger long on the summit of Cruachan. The way down is difficult at first, steep and over loose rock. It improves towards the bottom, where there is an opportunity to refresh hot feet in the cool waters of a lochan.

From the top of Meall Cuanail Ⓗ follow the fence which has led up from the lochan down to the track by the radio masts, and follow this to the dam (it is possible to cut a corner here by heading towards the western end of the dam before reaching the track, though the way down is quite difficult over tussocky grass). Follow the track away from the dam, without crossing the stream (the Allt Cruachan), but turn off to the right just before the bridge, by a wooden post, to retrace steps down the path to the railway and then back to the starting point.

Loch Awe

Ben More

Start	On shores of Loch na Keal opposite drive to Dhiseig Farm
Distance	6 miles (9.7km)
Approximate time	5 hours
Parking	Plenty of parking spaces beside loch
Refreshments	None
Ordnance Survey maps	Landranger 47 (Tobermory & North Mull), Explorer 375 (Isle of Mull East)

Ben More, which rises to 3171ft (966m) between Loch na Keal and Loch Scridain, is not only the highest peak on Mull but also the only one over 3000ft (914m) in the Inner Hebrides outside Skye. The ascent from the shores of Loch na Keal is steady and unremitting rather than strenuous, though there are some steep stretches and minor scrambles, and there is a clear path all the way. On the lower reaches the cascading burn of Abhainn Dhiseig makes an attractive sight, and from the higher parts, especially the summit, the views are magnificent, extending over much of the Western Highlands and Islands and including, in clear conditions, Ben Nevis and the Paps of Jura. It must be emphasised that on no account should this walk be attempted in bad weather, particularly during the winter, unless you are experienced and equipped for such conditions and able to navigate by using a compass.

Start by walking up the drive to Dhiseig Farm and just before the farm entrance, bear right and head up across grass to a metal gate **A**. Now begins the long and unrelenting climb to the summit of Ben More, steady rather than steep except in the latter stages.

After going through the gate, bear slightly right and continue beside the burn on the right – Abhainn Dhiseig – which flows through a narrow, wooded ravine over a series of waterfalls. Ahead are fine views of the prominent bulk of An Gearna and beyond it the distinctive, conical peak of Ben More.

Climb a stile, bear right and continue beside the burn, heading up through an attractive, rocky valley with more waterfalls. There is a series of cairns to mark the way, and these become more plentiful on the higher stages.

Ford the burn at a convenient spot **B** and continue more steeply above its right bank. The path bears right, away from the burn, and heads up to a ridge. After the path curves left comes the final, steep climb – with some easy scrambling in places – along the broad, stony ridge to the summit cone. The last $^{1}/_{4}$ mile (400m) to the cairn **C** is an easy

View from the summit of Ben More

and fairly level walk, with a sheer drop on the left.

From this 3171ft (966m) summit, there unfold the most magnificent, panoramic views of mountains, islands and sea lochs, encompassing the Western Highlands on the mainland, including Ben Nevis and Ben Cruachan, most of Mull, the Paps of Jura and the islands of Iona, Islay, Coll, Ulva and others. In exceptionally clear conditions the coast of Northern Ireland can sometimes be seen. More immediate is the narrow ridge which plunges steeply and spectacularly from the summit to the adjacent peak of A' Chìoch.

Retrace your steps down to the start, taking care on the first stages of the descent and enjoying more superb views, especially across Loch na Keal. ●

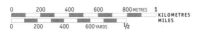

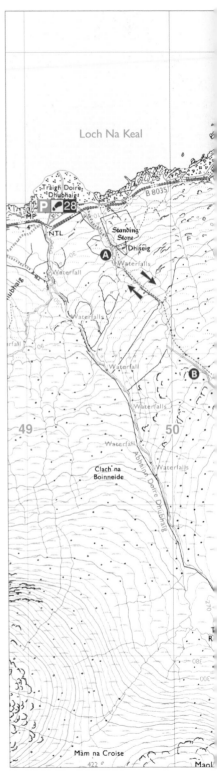

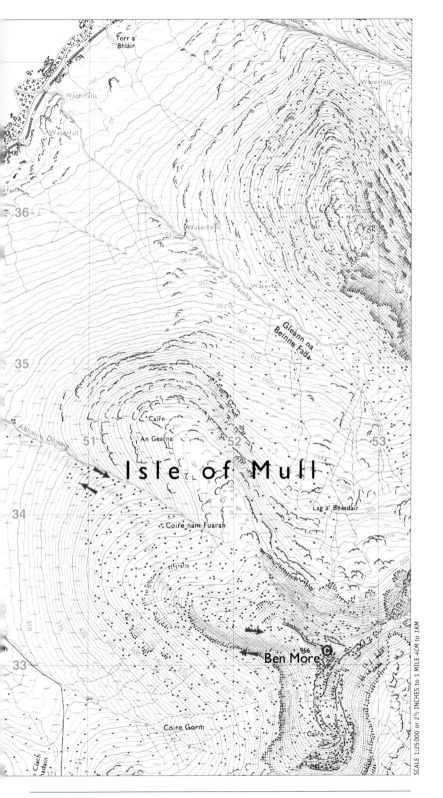

Isle of Mull

Forr a' Bhlàir

Waterfalls

Waterfall

Waterfalls

Abhainn na h-Uamha

Waterfall

Gleann na Beinne Fada

Cairn

An Gearna

Abhainn Dùiseig

Coire nam Fuaran

Lag a' Bhasdair

Ben More 966

Coire Gorm

Cairn

36

35

51 52 53

34

33

SCALE 1:25000 or 2½ INCHES to 1 MILE 4CM to 1KM

Further Information

 The Law and Tradition as they affect Walking in Scotland

Walkers following the routes given in this book should not run into problems, but it is as well to know something about the law as it affects access, and also something of the traditions which can be quite different in Scotland from elsewhere in Britain. Most of this is common sense, observing the country code and having consideration for other people and their activities which, after all, may be their livelihood.

It is often said that there is no law of trespass in Scotland. In fact there is, but the trespass itself is not usually a criminal offence. You can be asked to leave any property, and technically 'reasonable force' may be used to obtain your compliance – though the term is not defined! You can be charged with causing damage due to the trespass, but this would be hard to establish if you were just walking on open, wild, hilly country where, whatever the law, in practice there has been a long tradition of free access for recreational walking – something both the Scottish Landowners' Federation and the Mountaineering Council of Scotland do not want to see changed.

There are certain restrictions. Walkers should obey the country code and seasonal restrictions arising from lambing or stalking. Where there is any likelihood of such restrictions this is mentioned in the text and visitors are asked to comply. When camping, use a campsite. Camp fires should not be lit; they are a danger to moorland and forest, and really not necessary as lightweight and efficient stoves are now available.

Many of the walks in this book are on rights of way. The watchdog on rights of way in Scotland is the Scottish Rights of Way Society (SRWS), who maintain details on all established cases and will, if need be, contest attempted closures. They produce a booklet on the Scottish legal position *(Rights of Way, A Guide to the Law in Scotland, 1991)*, and their green signposts are a familiar sight by many footpaths and tracks, indicating the lines of historic routes.

In Scotland rights of way are not marked on Ordnance Survey maps as is the case south of the border. It was not felt necessary to show these as such on the maps – a further reflection of the freedom to roam that is enjoyed in Scotland. So a path on a map is no indication of a right of way, and many paths and tracks of great use to walkers were built by estates as stalking paths or for private access. While you may traverse such paths, taking due care to avoid damage to property and the natural environment, you should obey restricted access notices and leave if asked to do so.

The only established rights of way are those where a court case has resulted in a legal judgment, but there are thousands of other 'claimed' rights of way. Local planning authorities have a duty to protect rights of way – no easy task with limited resources. Many attempts at closing claimed rights of way have been successfully contested in the courts by the Scottish Rights of Way Society and local authorities.

A dog on a lead or under control may also be taken on a right of way. There is little chance of meeting a free-range solitary bull on any of the walks. Any herds seen are not likely to be dairy cattle, but all cows can be inquisitive and may approach walkers, especially if they have a dog. Dogs running among stock may be shot on the spot; this is not draconian legislation but a desperate attempt to stop sheep and lambs being harmed, driven to panic or lost, sometimes with fatal results. Any practical points or restrictions applicable will be made in the text of each walk. If there is no comment it can be assumed that the route carries no real restrictions.

Scotland in fact likes to keep everything as natural as possible, so, for instance, waymarking is kept to a minimum (the Scottish Rights of Way Society signposts and Forest Walk markers are in unobtrusive colours). In Scotland people are asked to 'walk softly in the wilderness, to take nothing except photographs, and leave nothing except footprints' – which is better than any law.

 ### Scotland's Hills and Mountains: a Concordat on Access

This remarkable agreement was published early in 1996 and is likely to have considerable influence on walkers' rights in Scotland in the future. The signatories include organisations which have formerly been at odds - the Scottish Landowners' Federation and the Ramblers' Association, for example. However they joined with others to make the Access Forum (a full list of signatories is detailed below). The RSPB and the National Trust for Scotland did not sign the Concordat initially but it is hoped that they will support its principles.

Oban

The signatories of the Concordat are:

Association of Deer Management Groups
Convention of Scottish Local Authorities
Mountaineering Council of Scotland
National Farmers' Union of Scotland
Ramblers' Association Scotland
Scottish Countryside Activities Council
Scottish Landowners' Federation
Scottish Natural Heritage
Scottish Sports Association
Scottish Sports Council

They agreed that the basis of access to the hills for the purposes of informal recreation should be:

- Freedom of access exercised with responsibility and subject to reasonable constraints for management and conservation purposes.
- Acceptance by visitors of the needs of land management, and understanding of how this sustains the livelihood, culture and community interests of those who live and work in the hills.
- Acceptance by land managers of the public's expectation of having access to the hills.
- Acknowledgment of a common interest in the natural beauty and special

St Oran's Chapel, Iona

qualities of Scotland's hills, and the need to work together for their protection and enhancement.

The Forum point out that the success of the Concordat will depend on all who manage or visit the hills acting on these four principles. In addition, the parties to the Concordat will promote good practice in the form of:

- Courtesy and consideration at a personal level.
- A welcome to visitors.
- Making advice readily available on the ground or in advance.
- Better information about the uplands and hill land uses through environmental education.
- Respect by visitors for the welfare needs of livestock and wildlife.
- Adherence to relevant codes and standards of good practice by visitors and land managers alike.
- Any local restrictions on access should be essential for the needs of management, should be fully explained, and be for the minimum period and area required.

Queries should be addressed to: Access Forum Secretariat, c/o Recreation and Access Branch, Scottish Natural Heritage, 2 Anderson Place, Edinburgh EH6 5NP.

 Safety on the Hills

The Highland hills and lower but remote areas call for care and respect. The idyllic landscape of the tourist brochures can change rapidly into a world of gales, rain and mist, potentially lethal for those ill-equipped or lacking navigational skills. The Scottish hills in winter can be arctic in severity, and even in summer, snow can lash the summits. It is essential that the walker is aware of these hazards, which are further discussed in the introduction.

At the very least carry adequate wind- and waterproof outer garments, food and drink to spare, a basic first-aid kit, whistle, map and compass – and know how to use them. Wear boots. Plan within your capabilities. If going alone ensure you leave details of your proposed route. Heed local advice, listen to weather forecasts, and do not hesitate to modify plans if conditions deteriorate.

Some of the walks in this book venture

into remote country and others climb high summits, and these walks should only be undertaken in good summer conditions. In winter they could well need the skills and experience of mountaineering rather than walking. In midwinter the hours of daylight are of course much curtailed, but given crisp, clear late-winter days many of the shorter expeditions would be perfectly feasible, if the guidelines given are adhered to. THINK is the only actual rule. Your life may depend on that. Seek to learn more about the Highlands and your part in them, and continue to develop your skills and broaden your experience.

Further Information

Glossary of Gaelic Names

Most of the place names in this region are Gaelic in origin, and this list gives some of the more common elements, which will allow readers to understand otherwise meaningless words and appreciate the relationship between place names and landscape features. Place names often have variant spellings, and the more common of these are given here.

aber	mouth of loch, river	eilidh	hind
abhainn	river	eòin, eun	bird
allt	stream	fionn	white
auch, ach	field	fraoch	heather
bal, bail, baile	town, homestead	gabhar, ghabhar, gobhar	goat
bàn	white, fair, pale	garbh	rough
bealach	hill pass	geal	white
beg, beag	small	ghlas, glas	grey
ben, beinn	hill	gleann, glen	narrow, valley
bhuidhe	yellow	gorm	blue, green
blar	plain	inbhir, inver	confluence
brae, braigh	upper slope, steepening	inch, inis, innis	island, meadow by river
breac	speckled	lag, laggan	hollow
cairn	pile of stones, often marking a summit	làrach	old site
		làirig	pass
cam	crooked	leac	slab
càrn	cairn, cairn-shaped hill	liath	grey
		loch	lake
caol, kyle	strait	lochan	small loch
ceann, ken, kin	head	màm	pass, rise
cil, kil	church, cell	maol	bald-shaped top
clach	stone	monadh	upland, moor
clachan	small village	mór, mor(e)	big
cnoc	hill, knoll, knock	odhar, odhair	dun-coloured
coille, killie	wood	rhu, rubha	point
corrie, coire, choire	mountain hollow	ruadh	red, brown
craig, creag	cliff, crag	sgòr, sgòrr, sgùrr	pointed
crannog, crannag	man-made island	sron	nose
dàl, dail	field, flat	stob	pointed
damh	stag	strath	valley (broader than glen)
dearg	red		
druim, drum	long ridge	tarsuinn	traverse, across
dubh, dhu	black, dark	tom	hillock (rounded)
dùn	hill fort	tòrr	hillock (more rugged)
eas	waterfall	tulloch, tulach	knoll
eilean	island	uisge	water, river

FURTHER INFORMATION ● 93

Mountain Rescue

In case of emergency the standard procedure is to dial 999 and ask for the police who will assess and deal with the situation.

First, however, render first aid as required and make sure the casualty is made warm and comfortable. The distress signal (six flashes/whistle-blasts, repeated at minute intervals) may bring help from other walkers in the area. Write down essential details: exact location (six-figure reference), time of accident, numbers involved, details of injuries, steps already taken; then despatch a messenger to phone the police.

If leaving the casualty alone, mark the site with an eye-catching object. Be patient; waiting for help can seem interminable.

 ## Useful Organisations

Association for the Protection of Rural Scotland
Gladstone's Land, 483 Lawnmarket, Edinburgh EH1 2NT
Tel. 0131 225 7012/3

Tràigh an t-Suidhe, Iona

Forestry Commission
Silvan House, 231 Corstorphine Road, Edinburgh EH12 7AT
Tel. 0131 334 0303

Historic Scotland
Longmore House, Salisbury Place, Edinburgh EH9 1SH
Tel. 0131 668 8600

Long Distance Walkers' Association
Bank House, High Street, Wrotham, Sevenoaks, Kent TN15 7AE
Tel. 01732 883705

Mountaineering Council of Scotland
The Old Granary, West Mill Street, Perth PH1 5QP
Tel. 01738 638227

Mountain Rescue Posts in the Southern Highlands
Arrochar Outdoor Centre: 01301 702998
Police Station, Crianlarich: 01838 300222
Dounans Camp School, Aberfoyle: 01877 382291

National Trust for Scotland
Wemyss House, 28 Charlotte Square, Edinburgh EH2 4ET
Tel. 0131 243 9300

Ordnance Survey
Romsey Road, Southampton SO16 4GU
Tel. 08456 05 05 05 (Lo-call)

Ramblers' Association (main office)
2nd Floor, Camelford House, 87–90 Albert
Embankment, London SE1 7TW
Tel. 020 7339 8500

Ramblers' Association (Scotland)
Kingfisher House, Auld Mart Business
Park, Milnathort, Kinross KY13 9DA
Tel. 01577 861222

Royal Society for the Protection of Birds
Abernethy Forest Reserve, Forest Lodge,
Nethybridge, Inverness-shire PH25 3EF
Tel. 01479 821409

Scottish Landowners' Federation
Stuart House, Eskmills Business Park,
Musselburgh, EH21 7PB
Tel. 0131 653 5400

Scottish Natural Heritage
12 Hope Terrace, Edinburgh, EH9 2AS
Tel. 0131 447 4784

Scottish Rights of Way Society Ltd
24 Annandale Street, Edinburgh EH7 4AN
Tel. 0131 558 1222

Scottish Wildlife Trust
Cramond House, Kirk Cramond, Cramond
Glebe Road, Edinburgh EH4 6NS
Tel. 0131 312 7765

Scottish Youth Hostels Association
7 Glebe Crescent, Stirling FK8 2JA
Tel. 0870 155 3255

www.visitscotland.com

Local tourist information offices:
Bowmore: 01496 810254
Campbeltown: 01586 552056
Craignure: 01680 812377
Inveraray: 01499 302063
Oban: 01631 563122
Tarbert: 01859 502011
Tobermory: 01688 302182

Weather forecasts
Mountaincall West Tel. 0891 500 441

Scotland seven-day forecast
Tel. 0891 112260
UK seven-day forecast Tel. 0891 333123

Ordnance Survey maps of Oban, Mull and Kintyre

Oban, Mull and Kintyre are covered by
Ordnance Survey 1:50 000 scale
($1\frac{1}{4}$ inches to 1 mile or 2cm to 1km)
Landranger map sheets 47, 48, 49, 50, 53,
55, 56, 60, 61, 63, 68 and 69. These all-
purpose maps are packed with information
to help you explore the area. Viewpoints,
picnic sites, places of interest and caravan
and camping sites are shown as well as
public rights of way information such as
footpaths and bridleways.

To examine Oban, Mull and Kintyre in
more detail, and especially if you are
planning walks, Ordnance Survey
Explorer maps at 1:25 000 scale ($2\frac{1}{2}$
inches to 1 mile or 4cm to 1km) are ideal:

352 (Islay South)

353 (Islay North)

355 (Jura & Scarba)

356 (Kintyre South)

358 (Loch Gilphead & Knapdale North)

359 (Oban, Kerrera & Loch Melfort)

360 (Loch Awe & Inveraray)

362 (Cowal West & Isle of Bute)

363 (Cowal East)

373 (Iona, Staffa & Ross of Mull)

374 (Isle of Mull North & Tobermory)

375 (Isle of Mull East)

376 (Oban & North Lorn)

377 (Loch Etive & Glen Orchy)

To get to Oban, Mull and Kintyre use the
Ordnance Survey Great Britain Travel
Map–Route at 1: 625 000 (1 inch to 10
miles or 4cm to 25km) scale or Ordnance
Survey Travel Map–Road 3 (Southern
Scotland and Northumberland) at
1:250 000 (1 inch to 4 miles or 1 cm to
2.5km) scale.

Ordnance Survey maps and guides are
available from most booksellers, stationers
and newsagents.

www.totalwalking.co.uk

www.totalwalking.co.uk
is the official website of the Jarrold
Pathfinder and Short Walks guides. This
interactive website features a wealth of
information for walkers – from the latest
news on route diversions and advice from
professional walkers to product news, free
sample walks and promotional offers.